Praise for Marie
and *Feng Shui Your Life*

"Marie Diamond is one of my spiritual teachers and she is really amazing. She has taught me to take my meditation to a whole other level. She has helped me to get the Feng Shui of my life in order, to organize myself better, to connect deeper with my Meditations and really, to get me where I am today."

BIG SEAN, MULTIPLE PLATINUM AWARD-WINNING ARTIST

"Marie Diamond's teachings have had a powerfully positive effect on my life. I have not only incorporated her wisdom in my personal life, but I have applied it in my film and television company. Marie brings infinite diamonds of wisdom in her teachings of Feng Shui, which are in harmony with the great laws and principles of the Universe."

RHONDA BYRNE, BEST-SELLING AUTHOR OF *THE SECRET*

"Marie Diamond is a great teacher, sage, master, and friend... We saw an immediate improvement in our business after her first consultation. Many good things have happened to my family and my business after her consultation and advice."

JACK CANFIELD, BEST-SELLING AUTHOR OF *THE SUCCESS PRINCIPLES* AND THE *CHICKEN SOUP FOR THE SOUL*™ SERIES

"Marie Diamond's work makes an immediate and astounding positive effect on your life. By the time she stepped onto my property and walked through the front door, she knew more about my life than most close friends. Within the short span of her consultation, her Diamond Feng Shui methods opened energy for harmony, health, and good fortune. Within the next few days and weeks, I saw increases in my income, my children experienced physical and emotional healing along with increased concentration and calm, and my wife averted a medical disaster. Seeing was believing!"

PAUL R. SCHEELE, CO-FOUNDER OF LEARNING STRATEGIES CORPORATION

"I met Marie Diamond through Jack Canfield in 2004. Soon she was in my home and office consulting on our Feng Shui energy. Opportunities began flooding in when we changed how the energy flowed around us. Within three months Entertainment Tonight showed one of our programs on TV, and in 2005 our profits increased 427%. I love Marie Diamond's book, *Feng Shui Your Life*, because it is an easy way for you to bring her principles to life. It is totally transformational."

"I want to thank you, Marie Diamond. Your Feng Shui has made such a big impact on my marriage, my family, and my business. What an inspiration you are – may you continue to enlighten this world and share your secret!"

"I first used the Marie Diamond App in my office and within nine weeks I had 20% more profits in my company. I thought it was a coincidence. Then we did the same thing to the office of my wife for her company and she had the same results. Within nine weeks she made 20% more income without doing anything else. I cannot say anything else than your system of Energy Numbers works!"

"Within one week of setting up my home to receive abundance under the direction of Marie Diamond, I received tens of thousands of dollars unexpectedly. And that was just the beginning! A continual stream of abundance now flows towards me in the most unexpected of ways. Marie's work is nothing short of miraculous."

FENG SHUI YOUR LIFE

FENG SHUI
YOUR
LIFE

A Beginner's Guide to Using
Your Home to Attract the
Life of Your Dreams

MARIE DIAMOND

HAY HOUSE

Carlsbad, California • New York City
London • Sydney • New Delhi

Published in the United Kingdom by:
Hay House UK Ltd, The Sixth Floor, Watson House
54 Baker Street, London W1U 7BU
Tel: +44 (0)20 3927 7290; Fax: +44 (0)20 3927 7291
www.hayhouse.co.uk

Published in the United States of America by:
Hay House Inc., PO Box 5100, Carlsbad, CA 92018-5100
Tel: (1) 760 431 7695 or (800) 654 5126
Fax: (1) 760 431 6948 or (800) 650 5115; www.hayhouse.com

Published in Australia by:
Hay House Australia Ltd, 18/36 Ralph St, Alexandria NSW 2015
Tel: (61) 2 9669 4299; Fax: (61) 2 9669 4144; www.hayhouse.com.au

Published in India by:
Hay House Publishers India, Muskaan Complex,
Plot No.3, B-2, Vasant Kunj, New Delhi 110 070
Tel: (91) 11 4176 1620; Fax: (91) 11 4176 1630; www.hayhouse.co.in

A catalogue record for this book is available from the British Library.

Tradepaper ISBN: 978-1-4019-7800-6
E-book ISBN: 978-1-83782-249-2
Audiobook ISBN: 978-1-83782-248-5

Interior images: Freepix, Shutterstock/Lucy Webster

10 9 8 7 6 5 4 3 2 1

Printed in the United States of America

This product uses papers sourced from responsibly managed forests. For
more information, see www.hayhouse.com.

I dedicate this book to all those who have sought out a better life for themselves through the use of Feng Shui. By following my teachings, it's my wish that you are all able to make your dream lives a reality.

CONTENTS

INTRODUCTION

What first comes to mind when you hear the term "Feng Shui"? Maybe it conjures up images of rearranging furniture, beige color schemes, and filling your home with money frogs for good luck.

No matter how you first heard about the term, there must have been something about Feng Shui that caught your attention and made you curious enough to find out more. That's where I come in! I am Marie Diamond, a globally recognized Feng Shui Master and creator of the Diamond Feng Shui School. Throughout this book, I will share with you the basic principles of Feng Shui in easy-to-follow steps. You will find a range of practical tasks designed to help you transform your home into a place that can help you attract money, love, and the life of your dreams.

Feng Shui has been a part of my life since I was 15 years old. I have spent the last 30 years traveling all over the world, teaching Feng Shui to people and consulting, and I have over one million online and in-person students. My list of Feng Shui clients includes top celebrities such as Steven Spielberg, Jason Bateman, Jodie Foster, and Big Sean, and best-selling authors like Vishen Lakhiani, Jack Canfield, John Gray, and Rhonda Byrne. I've advised CEOs from Fortune 500 companies, government officials, sports athletes, and even royal families!

What Does Feng Shui Mean?

Let's start at the beginning: What does Feng Shui mean exactly?

The words "Feng Shui" translate to "wind" and "water" in Chinese. Thousands of years ago, Chinese shamans would be called upon by the upper classes to find the best land for them to build on. The two most important things that the shamans would look out for were the right amounts of wind and water.

Any potential house would need to be sheltered from the harsh, cold winds that came whipping through the mountains, but with doors and windows still positioned in such a way as to allow the warm winds to pass through and air the house. The land would also need to be close to fresh, moving water in order to grow healthy crops, have transportation links to neighboring towns, and have clean water for bathing. Sounds sensible, right? By paying attention to this practical set of criteria, the shamans helped people to lead longer, healthier, and more successful lives, filled with good energy or "chi."

Feng Shui also takes into account the five elements of water, earth, fire, wood, and metal, making sure they're all represented and appropriately balanced in order to promote harmony within the home.

As the styles of buildings changed over the centuries, so did the ideas of Feng Shui. They became more detailed, focusing not just on the positioning of doors, windows, and the landscape but also on the interior layout of the home. Today, Feng Shui teaches people how to arrange their living space so as to attract this good energy into their lives.

How Did I Get into Feng Shui?

Ever since I was a child, I could feel energy. (Don't worry, this is by no means a requirement for studying Feng Shui!) I could detect the energy of people and places, and I was sensitive to the difference between positive and negative energy.

When I was growing up, there was one room in my childhood home where I felt negative energy. Unfortunately for me, it happened to be my bedroom. I always had nightmares there and sometimes I would even try to stay up late at night, reading with the sheets over my head, just so I didn't have to go to sleep. Not only was I very unhappy in this room, but I was also being bullied at school—it was almost as though the negative energy that was there was affecting other areas of my life.

Things came to a head when I was 15 and I was involved in a very serious accident, a near-death one in fact. I was hit by a speeding truck and the doctors informed me later that I had technically died at the scene, only to be brought back to life after many resuscitation attempts.

Recovery after the accident was long and grueling and, in an attempt to make sense of what had happened, I reached out to my spiritual mentor. I asked him what I had done wrong in order to attract such a horrible thing. What he said to me changed my life. Very simply, he told me, "Marie, you have bad Feng Shui." He went on to tell me that if I switched bedrooms, I would see a dramatic improvement.

At that time, my older brothers had already moved out of the house, so I quickly moved into their old bedroom. I gave the room a fresh coat of bright orange paint. I changed the position of my bed and I made sure my desk was facing my Success Direction. I started drawing pictures of myself surrounded by friends, and hung these up all around me.

Within just two weeks, I got my first boyfriend and suddenly the boring, lonely girl that I had been blossomed into a vibrant, popular one. The teenagers who had previously ignored and bullied me were now paying attention to me, and I attracted a group of incredible friends. My life was filled with so much joy, fun, and laughter; a complete contrast to what it had been like before. Something had definitely shifted, but I hadn't changed my looks, what I was thinking, or even how I was behaving. In fact, the only thing that I had changed was my environment. It was then I truly understood the power of Feng Shui.

What Is Diamond Feng Shui?

There are many different types of Feng Shui: Compass Feng Shui, Ba Gua Feng Shui, and more. Diamond Feng Shui is the unique system that I created by combining traditional classical Feng Shui teachings with the Law of Attraction, neuroscience, and quantum physics principles. Stay with me—it's much simpler than it sounds!

Feng Shui enables you to increase the good, abundant energy in your home, be it a studio apartment or a five-bedroom mansion, in order to improve the lives of those living in it.

In Feng Shui, there is the principle that each person's fortune is the sum of three different kinds of equally important luck—Heaven Luck, Human Luck, and Earth Luck:

♦ **Heaven Luck** refers to the life circumstances you were born into—your family, culture, and your physical abilities. These tend to be things that can't easily be changed. Some view this as the path that God has chosen for you, your soul purpose, or refer to it as your destiny or karma.

- **Human Luck** refers to your attitude, behavior, your mindset, and the choices you make every day that affect your life. It's the focus of most self-help books: the idea that changing your thoughts and feelings will change your life. It goes without saying that a positive and grateful attitude is important, but it requires a lot of time, practice, and discipline to learn to think that way. If you've ever had a bad day, you know how tough it can be to force yourself to look on the bright side!

- **Earth Luck** refers to changing your environment to improve the good "chi," or energy, around you. It stands to reason that if your home is in chaos with clutter and dust, it's harder to attract positive energy into your life. Similarly, if your house is unwelcoming, how can you expect good things to want to find you? Happily, Earth Luck is the easiest and quickest to improve; all it takes is some basic knowledge and a little work.

By using Feng Shui to improve your Earth Luck, you'll discover that your Human Luck improves too; you'll find yourself with a more positive attitude and a more upbeat outlook on life. It'll also improve your Heaven Luck, meaning that you'll find it easier to find and live out your true soul purpose.

Clearing Up Misconceptions

A common misunderstanding about Feng Shui is that it's a type of magic, or a part of a specific religion. I'm happy to say that this couldn't be farther from the truth! Feng Shui is an energy practice that can be used alongside any religious belief, meaning you're perfectly safe to study it alongside your own religious or spiritual practices.

If you're having trouble figuring out how Feng Shui can fit in your life alongside your religion, try thinking of it as a self-care activity. It's about creating a safe, inviting, and peaceful home for yourself while also maximizing the good energy in it. Feng Shui helps you to create the environment that you want in order to attract the life that you desire.

Another misconception about Feng Shui is that you need to spend a lot of money. However, repainting walls, buying new furniture, filling your home with expensive crystals—none of this is necessary. I believe that Feng Shui is most effective when you make the most of what you already have. Whether it's learning how to best sort away any clutter, giving your rooms a thorough dusting and closets a complete sort through, or buying some colorful candles from your local store, Feng Shui can be practiced at any budget. All you need is a little creativity!

How to Use This Book

This book is divided into different chapters, making it easy for you to dip in and out of. The book begins with the basic background information about Feng Shui and the ideas behind it. Once you've read that, you'll find chapters on how to use Feng Shui to help attract different outcomes, such as improved family relationships or a more successful career. Finally, you'll find the Feng Shui dos and don'ts for each room in the home.

This book was written to be a one-stop source for all your Feng Shui needs and one that you can refer back to whenever you need to. It's my hope that this book will follow you throughout your life when you move home, move in with a partner, or travel across the world.

While the advice in this book is aimed at those new to Feng Shui and is intended to be as accessible as possible, you may find that some of the tips seem a little strange at first. If you're unsure about a particular change you've made, I would recommend sticking with it for at least nine days and then seeing how you feel. It takes about nine days to notice the positive effects that changing the flow of energy can bring, and when the time comes, I'm sure you'll enjoy your newfound energy so much that you won't want to change things back!

With that in mind, let's take the first step on your Feng Shui journey. Begin by downloading the free Marie Diamond app and entering in your details. The app will then tell you your Personal Energy Number (you'll need this later!), your Energy Archetype, and your four Personal Directions in accordance with Feng Shui.

You can scan the QR code below, which will take you to the Marie Diamond app in your app store:

CHAPTER 1

Analyze Your Energy Flow

This first step is all about checking in on how the energy of your life is at the moment and figuring out which areas need the most attention. What do you want Feng Shui to help you with? What kind of life do you want to have? What would you keep from your life as it is now, and what would you change?

To help you, I've created an Energy Quiz to figure out the current state of your life. For each question, you'll need to circle a number from 1 to 9. In this scale, 1 represents extreme negative and 9 represents extreme positive.

For example, for a question that says: "How is your money situation right now?" answering 9 would mean that your current money situation is absolutely perfect;

you have all the money you could possibly need and there isn't a single thing you would change. Answering 1 would suggest a lot of anxiety over your current situation, perhaps in the form of debt, struggling to pay your bills, and generally seeing money as a source of stress. Realistically, your answer will likely fall in between those two figures.

Question 1: Your Money

How is your money situation right now?

1   2   3   4   5   6   7   8   9

Question 2: Your Self-Esteem

Do you consider yourself to be a confident person?

1   2   3   4   5   6   7   8   9

Question 3: Your Relationships

Do you feel satisfied in your relationships with your partner, friends, family, and colleagues?

1   2   3   4   5   6   7   8   9

Question 4: Your Purpose

Do you feel you're finding time to follow your passions and be creative?

1   2   3   4   5   6   7   8   9

Question 5: Your Support System

Do you feel you have enough support from the people in your life?

1   2   3   4   5   6   7   8   9

Question 6: Your Career

Do you feel satisfied in your professional life?

1   2   3   4   5   6   7   8   9

Question 7: Your Spirituality

Do you make time for spiritual connections in your life, either through meditation, prayer, or by being part of a religious community?

1   2   3   4   5   6   7   8   9

Question 8: Your Health

How would you rate your current physical, emotional, and mental health?

1   2   3   4   5   6   7   8   9

Question 9: Your Time

Do you feel you have balance in your life?

1   2   3   4   5   6   7   8   9

Once you've finished answering, add up all the numbers to find your overall score:

Less than 36: Your Life Needs Urgent Attention

If you scored less than 36 in total, you need an urgent energy shift! Focus on the questions where you scored less than 3 and make those areas a priority for change. You're in desperate need of a life change, so you should get started with the next chapters as soon as possible.

Between 36 and 60: Your Life Needs an Upgrade

If you scored between 36 and 60, your energy is quite good, but there are still areas that need some care. If there were any questions where you scored less than 5, turn your attention to those first and keep them in mind as you make your way through the next chapters.

Above 60: Your Life Is Right on Track

If you scored between 61 and 81, congratulations— there's a lot of really positive energy in your life! Look at any questions where you scored less than 7 if you want to make any small adjustments or improvements. You're in a really powerful place to begin your Feng Shui journey, so make sure to keep your journey on track.

CHAPTER 2

Becoming Mindful of Your Home

In order to know what it is you have to improve on in your home, you must first know what it is you're working with. You began by taking an inventory of your life, so now it's time to take a look at your home.

Since we spend so much of our life in our home, we can sometimes become blind to the clutter, the mess, and the unfinished repairs that surround us. To help with this, here's a very simple mindfulness exercise to enable you look at your home with fresh, new eyes.

With a pencil, notepad, and this book in hand, stand outside your home, either on the sidewalk or in the hallway of your apartment building. Close your eyes and take a few deep breaths. When you open your eyes, you're going to pretend that this isn't your home anymore. You're a real estate agent; this is your latest property and you're doing your first walk-through.

Look at your front door as if you've never seen it before. Open it and then walk slowly through the rooms, taking your time to really look around. What's inside the drawers and cupboards? What are the windows like, or the furniture, or decor? How does being in each room make you feel?

Don't be afraid to be critical since this step requires that you be completely honest. It doesn't matter if your rooms are piled high with junk; this isn't the time for shame, just honesty.

As you walk through each room in your home, consider the following questions:

♦   Is there anything here that needs to be fixed or repaired?

♦   Is there anything here that can be donated or gotten rid of?

♦   Is there anything missing from this room that you don't have?

♦ Is this room messy?

♦ Does this room have enough storage space?

♦ Have you upgraded this space within the last year?

♦ Do you feel good here?

♦ Would you feel comfortable bringing a guest here?

Since this is just a simple mindfulness exercise, you don't need to find any solutions just yet. That will come later; for now, a simple "yes" or "no" is all that's needed! Write your answers in your notepad, so you can refer back to them later.

CHAPTER 3

Writing Your
Feng Shui Goals

It's time now to think about your Feng Shui goals more specifically. You've finished taking a general inventory of your life, meaning you have the perfect foundation for writing down exactly what it is you want to achieve with Feng Shui.

Goal writing can be a very powerful tool, but there are guidelines you should follow in order for them to be as effective as possible.

Write Your Goals in the Present Tense

When writing down your goals, make sure that they're written in the present tense and begin with "I am...."

Avoid using "I will...," "I'm going to...," or phrases like "if I..." or "when I...."

It might seem a little strange to write down something you want to achieve as if you've already achieved it, but it's the most effective way to make your goals a reality.

Here are a couple of examples to get you started:

♦ Instead of "I will get a job that pays twice my previous salary," try "I am in a job that pays twice my previous salary," or "I am attracting a job with a salary that better reflects my worth."

♦ Instead of "I will lose weight," try "I am making healthy substitutions in my diet, setting time aside daily for exercise, and enjoying my new, slimmer figure."

Choose Positive Language Over Negative Language

Goals should always state what it is you *do* want, not what you *don't* want. We don't want to confuse our subconscious mind. If you load up on negative language, this will seep into your subconscious and become your focus, whether you want it to or not. It's like the old adage that says if someone tells you "don't think about an elephant," the first thing you immediately do is to think about an elephant, even though you were just told not to!

Here are examples of using positive language over negative language:

♦ Instead of "I'm no longer stuck in my boring, dead-end job," try "I am working at a fulfilling, engaging job that has plenty of room for progression."

♦ Instead of "I'm not getting into relationships with a partner who wastes my time and treats me like dirt," try "I am enjoying being in the company of a partner who values me and treats me like royalty."

The Goal Has to Be Measurable and Testable

How can you know if you've achieved a goal if there's no checklist to measure it against? When goal writing, it helps to be as specific as possible so that you can pinpoint the exact moment your goal is achieved. Numbers, deadlines, and exact criteria are all helpful to include because they make the goals more specific.

It also helps to avoid broad terms like "rich," "happy," or "healthy," because these things can mean lots of different things to different people. What "rich" looks like to a

CEO already on a $5 million salary is very different from what it looks like to a student working a minimum wage job. Once again, be as specific as you can in what these things mean to you.

Examples of measurable and testable goals include:

♦ Instead of "I am happy," try "I am spending at least five hours of quality time with my family each week."

♦ Instead of "I am rich," try "I am attracting enough money each month to pay all my bills, add $500 to my savings, donate to charity, and treat myself to delicious restaurant meals and weekend trips away whenever I want."

Make Sure Your Goals Are Worthwhile

These are your own personal goals for you and you alone. Ignore what goals you think you *should* be making, or which ones your friends, family, or even society would want you to make. If your heart isn't really in your goals, you won't have the passion needed to make them a reality and you'll only end up with a sense of guilt over 1) not achieving them and 2) not even wanting to achieve them in the first place.

Once you've written down your goals, read back over them. If you don't feel a little spark of excitement deep inside you, you might need to have a rethink about whether this is really the goal for you.

For example:

♦   Instead of "I am living my parents' dream of being married with two children," try "I am surrounded by a family of my own choosing. I travel the world and create unforgettable memories wherever I go."

♦   Instead of "I am living the kind of life that social media tells me I should be living," try "I am living a life that I am passionate about."

EXERCISE

Now that you know the rules, grab a notepad and write down your top five goals. Write them in order of priority, and don't be afraid to think big!

Once you've written your goals, you can start to see the sorts of things that you want to attract with the help of Feng Shui. You might find that your goals have certain recurring themes, like improving your relationship with your family or making your business a success. Keep your goals in mind as you work your way through this book, so that you can pay close attention to the chapters that explain how to activate your home and attract the outcomes you desire.

CHAPTER 4

The Importance of Space Clearing

You've completed the initial planning stage, so now's the time to roll up your sleeves and get to work!

The first step is something we refer to as *space clearing* in Feng Shui, which simply refers to mindfully sorting through all your stuff to see what you want to keep, what you need to repair, and which items you don't want or need anymore.

Why is this important? The first and most practical reason is that it's easier to feel relaxed in a clean and organized home. If you're having to wade through junk every time you open your closet, or if you waste time each morning trying to hunt down your car keys amongst the mess in your living room, do you think that's going to put you in the best mood to start your day? Mess can be a source of stress, so getting rid of it is just one thing you can do to make your life a little easier.

Secondly, Feng Shui teaches us that energy must be able to move and flow freely throughout the home. Unnecessary clutter disrupts this flow and can result in the energy becoming stale and lifeless. Chaos in the home equals chaos in the mind, and space clearing is one way we can ensure the energy in our home stays fresh and positive.

How Do I Start?

Space clearing is something that's best done during the daytime. As tempting as it may be to start sorting through cupboards late at night when there are no distractions or people to bother you, space clearing can bring up some powerful emotions that can leave you feeling restless. Doing it when the sun is out and your rooms are still light and airy will help to keep you in a sunny, upbeat mood.

To avoid overwhelming yourself, stick to clearing one room or one area (such as a closet or your kitchen pantry) at a time. Once you start space clearing a room or area, make sure you finish it that day. Going to bed with your home still in disarray might be tempting, but you may find that your motivation has gone the next day and you're making excuses not to finish what you've started!

You can use the checklist you made back in Chapter 2 as a guide: Which rooms stuck out as needing extra attention? Begin with these rooms and then work your way through the rest of your home.

Whichever room you choose to start in, begin by spraying some lavender-scented air mist. If there are areas of the room (particularly enclosed spaces such as closets) that haven't been visited in a while, the air can get stuffy. The mist helps to freshen things up and lighten the air, meaning you can work without any unpleasant odors!

Then, get five boxes or bags:

♦   Box 1: items you want to keep.

♦   Box 2: broken items that need to be thrown away.

♦   Box 3: items you no longer use, but which can be passed on to your family or friends.

♦   Box 4: items you want to donate to charity.

♦   Box 5: items you want to sell, at a consignment store or online, for example.

Go through your drawers, cupboards, bookcases, and closets and place everything inside them in one of the five boxes. Be practical—when was the last time you used this item? Does it serve a particular purpose; is it solving a problem that you have in your life? Is it practical, beautiful, or sentimental to you, or is it just something that you've forgotten about? A quick and easy way to decide what stays and what goes is to ask yourself whether you're going to use this item in the next year. If it's a no, strongly consider getting rid of it.

> **Piles of magazines or newspapers can quickly become clutter if left unattended. Set out three boxes: one for interesting articles, one for recipes, and one for coupons. Tear out the relevant pages from your magazines and newspapers, and then recycle whatever's left.**

Now, it could be the case that the majority of things you have *do* serve a purpose for you and there might only be a few things that you really want to get rid of—and that's perfectly fine! Feng Shui isn't about throwing away all your possessions in favor of a minimalist approach; we just need to double-check we're not adding unnecessary clutter to our lives.

Once you've gone through everything, give the space a good dusting. As for air mist, cleaning products that contain lavender oil are great for purifying the energy of a room, plus the smell will help you unwind after all that hard work! Vacuum the carpets, shake out any rugs, and open up the windows to let in some fresh air. Place the items that you've decided to keep back in their correct place. Hang up all your clothes neatly in your closet, making sure that everything is clean and laundered.

Looking back on your checklist from Chapter 2, there may also be some repairs you need to make. Things like broken drawers, clogged drains, or loose doorknobs can also affect the positive energy of a home. Make a list of all the repairs that need to be made, whether they're quick, easy things you can do yourself, or jobs that perhaps require the skills of a professional handyperson. Try putting a sticker on items that need fixing as a reminder of what needs to be done. Once the item is repaired, simply peel off the sticker.

Your Space-Clearing Buddy

If you live with other people, either family members or roommates, encourage them to get involved too.

Having a space-clearing buddy is wonderful because it means that you can encourage each other to stay focused on the task at hand. You can hold each other accountable and push each other to make those hard decisions.

How Often Should I Be Space Clearing?

Once you've done your initial space clearing at the start of your Feng Shui journey, you should aim to do it at least twice a year: once at the beginning of the year (anytime from the start of January to the end of March) and once nearer the end (anytime from the start of September to the end of November). It's important to make sure that you're not space clearing on the day of the Chinese New Year or your own birthday, though, since any sort of cleaning or tidying on those days can "sweep" away all your good luck for the year.

> Make sure to declutter your computer and mobile phone too. Delete or archive old files, emails, and text messages. Is your voicemail filled with old messages? Take time to clear it and no doubt those long-awaited calls you've been expecting will start to come in.

In general, space clearing can be done anytime you feel "stuck." If you're having troubles with your relationship, clear out your bedroom. If you feel like you're not progressing in your career, clear out your office or desk. It's a great tool to use anytime you feel in need of change.

CHAPTER 5

The Power Position

Now that you've cleared the clutter, it's time to learn about one of the most important basic principles of Feng Shui: *the power position.*

It is exactly what it sounds like: It's the way you position yourself in your space so that you're the most powerful in the room. You want to tell the world that you view yourself as the king, queen, or president of your home!

EXERCISE

As a quick exercise, think carefully about any photo you've ever seen of someone sitting in the power position in a room. Maybe it's the President of the United States sitting in the Oval Office, the King of

England sitting on his throne, or even a CEO sitting in a conference room. Think about where in the room they're sitting, what kind of chair they're sitting on, and the location of everyone around them. What does this tell us about their status? How does this show that they are the most important person in the room?

In order to sit in a power position, there are a set of rules to follow and these rules are the same for everyone.

Face the Main Door of the Room

The first and most important rule of the power position is that you must be able to see the main door into the room (i.e. the door that you walk through to enter the room). The door can be in your peripheral vision but you must be able to see it without having to turn your head.

This is beneficial on a number of levels. With regard to evolution, our early ancestors faced a lot of danger in their lives, so they had to be completely aware of their surroundings in order to survive. Think about the cavemen who had to guard their families against wild animal attacks! So, with that in mind, it makes sense to have a clear view of your door so that you know exactly who's coming into the room.

Secondly, in terms of Feng Shui, you want to make sure you're in the path of the incoming flow of positive energy. You want to be able to see all the good opportunities that enter through the door, and you want to make sure you're making yourself available to any good fortune that comes knocking!

Let's look at each room to explain how the power position works.

The Office

The first rule is (you've guessed it!) to have your desk positioned so that you're facing the door when you're sitting down.

Next, try to position your desk so that there is a solid wall behind you. It's very important that you don't have your desk facing a wall as this means that you'll have your back to the room.

From a business viewpoint, how can you feel like a valued member of a team if you're facing away from all the action? You want to be sat so that you're part of the action, not so that things are happening quite literally behind your back. It's easier to collaborate and work well as a team when people are able to face each other directly from their desks, not when they're staring at the back of someone's head.

Thirdly, you want to make sure there is at least 3ft to 10ft (roughly 1m to 3m) of space between you and the door. Having a nice amount of open space in front of you helps to improve the flow of incoming energy and allows the Universe to help you manifest what it is you desire.

If you often have meetings in your office with potential clients or business partners, try to have enough space in front of your desk to place a chair there, too. After all, what's more encouraging to those you wish to do business with than having a ready space for them to sit? Even if your business is entirely online and you don't have clients come to your office, it's still a symbol that you are welcoming them and their business into your space.

Lastly, make sure your office chair is supportive enough for you. Think of the President's chair in the Oval Office or the King of England's throne—these chairs have a lot of things in common. They're both high-backed chairs with neck support and armrests. In order to activate your power position, you too must feel like you're sitting on a throne! Head down to an office supply store and try out the different chairs they have until you find the most comfortable and supportive one for you.

Now, a common question I get is how to activate your power position if you share an office with lots of people. As a general rule, the receptionist, secretary, or admin assistants would be the ones sat closest to the door and the most senior members of the team (like the CEO, manager, or team leader) will be sat farthest away from the door. If you work in an office with a fixed floor plan that stops you from being able to move your desk to face the door, just hang up a small mirror that allows you to get a view of the door from wherever you're sitting.

The Living Room

In much the same way, you want to make sure that the main sofa in the living room is positioned in such a way that you can see the main door to the room without having to turn your neck.

Now, this can be a bit tricky if you have a living room that's smaller in size: Placing the sofa in the power position could mean cutting off a huge chunk of the room! If that is the case, try to position the sofa as best as you can, and then have an armchair facing the door instead. Since armchairs are smaller, they're easier to position without having to sacrifice too much floor space.

As before, try to leave at least 3ft (roughly 1m) of space between the sofa or armchair and the door.

If you have guests coming over, it's still important that you take a seat with a view of the door. You might be tempted to offer up the best seat in the room, but this is your home and your space; you deserve to be the most powerful person there!

The Bedroom

Firstly, you want to make sure that your bed is positioned so that when you wake up and sit straight up, you're facing the main door. Remember, the door in question will be the main door to the bedroom that leads out into the hallway, not the closet or bathroom door. You want to make sure that, when you're in bed, you can comfortably see it without having to twist your body or turn your head. Try to ensure that you're leaving a fair amount of space between your bed and the door—anywhere from 3ft to 10ft (roughly 1m to 3m) of space is best.

Secondly, make sure that the head of your bed is pushed up against a wall. You want there to be as little space as possible between the headboard and the wall. As strange as it may sound, I've encountered people who place their bed in the center of their room, with walking space all around it—this is definitely a big Feng Shui no-no! To maintain the power position, you need there to be a wall behind you while you sleep. If you have a window behind you, invest in thick curtains to block out the moonlight. Having the moon shine in on you can lead to a poor night's sleep.

Thirdly, you need to ensure that your bed frame is supportive and has a solid, sturdy headboard. Pick one that's either upholstered or made from solid wood. You want to make sure that when you're sitting up in bed, you're not just sitting up against the wall. Not only does this benefit you in a practical way but it has important Feng Shui benefits, too. A supportive bed frame will help ground your energy, while a sturdy headboard means that you can sit up in bed and feel protected. A headboard with slats can leave you feeling less than energized in the morning, not to mention the fact that they can be very uncomfortable to sit up against! If you do have a headboard with slats, cover these with fabric or extra pillows until you're able to purchase a better, more supportive headboard.

Out and About

Whether you're at a restaurant, a coffee shop, or even a parent–teacher conference, you can still apply some of the rules for the power position. Try to ensure that you pick a seat that's facing the main door of the room you're in and don't be afraid to ask for a new chair if you find yourself sitting on one that's broken or wobbly.

What If I'm Not Able to Face the Door?

Ideally, all it would take is a little creative thinking and some time spent rearranging furniture before you found a floor plan that allowed you to face the door. However, we all know that it can be tricky in rooms with narrow walls or sloping ceilings!

So, if there's absolutely no way you're able to move your bed or desk to face the door, hang a small mirror across from the door instead. Then, position your bed or desk so that you can see the mirror. This way, you'll still be able to see the people coming in and out of the room.

❝ *In my very first job, I sat with my back to everyone in the office. I was having trouble feeling like I was a part of the team and every time I wanted to show my work to my manager, she'd have already passed behind me before I'd even noticed she was there. I was struggling to get my work recognized and people in the office were starting to talk behind my back.*

One morning, I decided to go to the office early to look for an empty table. I set up my desk at a new table in a position that meant I could actually see everyone in the room! Every time the manager passed me now, I could easily flag her down and say, "Here, the file is ready," or "I have an idea about that new project." It wasn't that I was working any harder than I normally did, but my contributions were finally being recognized.

I found out that the previous employees who had sat at my old desk had all left within a few months of starting, which didn't surprise me. I had been ready to quit too, but after moving my desk, I went on to be offered a promotion in just six short months and replaced my manager. **❞**

CHAPTER 6

Your Personal Energy Number

One of the unique things about Feng Shui is that it doesn't give you a single, one-size-fits-all approach. Since everybody is different, it makes sense that the energy flows differently for them in their home. For this reason, Feng Shui takes into account something called your Personal Energy Number.

This number is calculated using a special mathematical formula that is different from the traditional "adding up" method of numerology. Your Personal Energy Number is a number from 1 to 9 and is based on your date of birth and the sex you were assigned with at birth. If you're transgender, you can choose to use your affirmed gender and a special date that is closely linked with your gender identity (for example, the date you first became aware of your gender identity, the date you came out to your loved ones, or the date you first began any gender-affirming medical procedures).

Each Energy Number represents a different Energy Archetype—similar to how each different astrological sign comes with a different set of personality traits. Your Energy Number will also tell you your four best Personal Directions, which are where the energy in your home is the most powerful for you. There are different Personal Directions for attracting success and money, good health, good relationships, and wisdom and personal growth.

By taking your Personal Energy Number into account, you'll be able to use this good luck energy to attract the things you want with better and quicker results.

How Do I Find Out My Personal Energy Number?

Simply head to the free Marie Diamond app and enter your details—you can scan the QR code in the Introduction section of this book. The app will then tell you your Personal Energy Number, your archetype, and your four Personal Directions according to Feng Shui. If you don't have access to a smartphone, no need to worry! If you were born after 1950, just locate your birthday in the table on the following pages to find your Personal Energy Number:

Year	Birthday	Male	Female
1950	Feb 17, 1950–Feb 5, 1951	5	1
1951	Feb 6, 1951–Jan 26, 1952	4	2
1952	Jan 27, 1952–Feb 13, 1953	3	3
1953	Feb 14, 1953–Feb 2, 1954	2	4
1954	Feb 3, 1954–Jan 23, 1955	1	5
1955	Jan 24, 1955–Feb 11, 1956	9	6
1956	Feb 12, 1956–Jan 30, 1957	8	7
1957	Jan 31, 1957–Feb 17, 1958	7	8
1958	Feb 18, 1958–Feb 7, 1959	6	9
1959	Feb 8, 1959–Jan 27, 1960	5	1
1960	Jan 28, 1960–Feb 14, 1961	4	2
1961	Feb 15, 1961–Feb 4, 1962	3	3
1962	Feb 5, 1962–Jan 24, 1963	2	4
1963	Jan 25, 1963–Feb 12, 1964	1	5
1964	Feb 13, 1964–Feb 1, 1965	9	6
1965	Feb 2, 1965–Jan 20, 1966	8	7
1966	Jan 21, 1966–Feb 8, 1967	7	8
1967	Feb 9, 1967–Jan 29, 1968	6	9
1968	Jan 30, 1968–Feb 16, 1969	5	1
1969	Feb 17, 1969–Feb 5, 1970	4	2

Year	Birthday	Male	Female
1970	Feb 6, 1970–Jan 26, 1971	3	3
1971	Jan 27, 1971–Feb 14, 1972	2	4
1972	Feb 15, 1972–Feb 2, 1973	1	5
1973	Feb 3, 1973–Jan 22, 1974	9	6
1974	Jan 23, 1974–Feb 10, 1975	8	7
1975	Feb 11, 1975–Jan 30, 1976	7	8
1976	Jan 31, 1976–Feb 17, 1977	6	9
1977	Feb 18, 1977–Feb 6, 1978	5	1
1978	Feb 7, 1978–Jan 27, 1979	4	2
1979	Jan 28, 1979–Feb 15, 1980	3	3
1980	Feb 16, 1980–Feb 4, 1981	2	4
1981	Feb 5, 1981–Jan 24, 1982	1	5
1982	Jan 25, 1982–Feb 12, 1983	9	6
1983	Feb 13, 1983–Feb 1, 1984	8	7
1984	Feb 2, 1984–Feb 19, 1985	7	8
1985	Feb 20, 1985–Feb 8, 1986	6	9
1986	Feb 9, 1986–Jan 28, 1987	5	1
1987	Jan 29, 1987–Feb 16, 1988	4	2
1988	Feb 17, 1988–Feb 5, 1989	3	3
1989	Feb 6, 1989–Jan 26, 1990	2	4
1990	Jan 27, 1990–Feb 14, 1991	1	5
1991	Feb 15, 1991–Feb 3, 1992	9	6
1992	Feb 4, 1992–Jan 22, 1993	8	7

Year	Birthday	Male	Female
1993	Jan 23, 1993–Feb 9, 1994	7	8
1994	Feb 10, 1994–Jan 30, 1995	6	9
1995	Jan 31, 1995–Feb 18, 1996	5	1
1996	Feb 19, 1996–Feb 6, 1997	4	2
1997	Feb 7, 1997–Jan 27, 1998	3	3
1998	Jan 28, 1998–Feb 15, 1999	2	4
1999	Feb 16, 1999–Feb 4, 2000	1	5
2000	Feb 5, 2000–Jan 23, 2001	9	6
2001	Jan 24, 2001–Feb 11, 2002	8	7
2002	Feb 12, 2002–Jan 31, 2003	7	8
2003	Feb 1, 2003–Jan 21, 2004	6	9
2004	Jan 22, 2004–Feb 8, 2005	5	1
2005	Feb 9, 2005–Jan 28, 2006	4	2
2006	Jan 29, 2006–Feb 17, 2007	3	3
2007	Feb 18, 2007–Feb 6, 2008	2	4
2008	Feb 7, 2008–Jan 25, 2009	1	5
2009	Jan 26, 2009–Feb 13, 2010	9	6
2010	Feb 14, 2010–Feb 2, 2011	8	7
2011	Feb 3, 2011–Jan 22, 2012	7	8
2012	Jan 23, 2012–Feb 9, 2013	6	9
2013	Feb 10, 2013–Jan 30, 2014	5	1
2014	Jan 31, 2014–Feb 18, 2015	4	2
2015	Feb 19, 2015–Feb 7, 2016	3	3

Year	Birthday	Male	Female
2016	Feb 8, 2016–Jan 27, 2017	2	4
2017	Jan 28, 2017–Feb 15, 2018	1	5
2018	Feb 16, 2018–Feb 4, 2019	9	6
2019	Feb 5, 2019–Jan 24, 2020	8	7
2020	Jan 25, 2020–Feb 11, 2021	7	8
2021	Feb 11, 2021–Jan 31, 2022	6	9
2022	Feb 1, 2022–Jan 21, 2023	5	1
2023	Jan 22, 2023–Feb 9, 2024	4	2
2024	Feb 10, 2024–Jan 28, 2025	3	3
2025	Jan 29, 2025–Feb 16, 2026	2	4
2026	Feb 17, 2026–Feb 5, 2027	1	5
2027	Feb 6, 2027–Jan 25, 2028	9	6
2028	Jan 26, 2028–Feb 12, 2029	8	7
2029	Feb 13, 2029–Feb 2, 2030	7	8
2030	Feb 3, 2030–Jan 22, 2031	6	9

Just to give you two examples, if you're a man born on February 16, 1999, your Personal Energy Number would be 1. If you're a woman born on February 14, 1991, your Personal Energy Number would be 5.

Once you've found your Personal Energy Number, look in the list below to learn more about it, including its

Energy Archetype, your Personal Directions, and even the names of a few celebrities who share your number. Each Energy Number represents a direction on the compass, but since there are eight compass directions and nine Energy Numbers, Energy Number 5 represents the center. More than a thousand years ago, the Feng Shui Masters made the decision to include both a male and female version of Energy Number 5 as a way to bring balance to this system.

Personal Energy Number 1

Archetype: The Wealth Creator

You seek fortune in all of the projects in your life, for yourself and those around you. Being with your family will bring you peace. In your search for recognition, start by recognizing what it is you're capable of. Your spiritual journey is one rooted in reflection.

♦ Success Direction: Southeast

♦ Health Direction: East

♦ Relationship Direction: South

♦ Wisdom Direction: North

♦ Celebrities with this Energy Number: Andy Warhol, Elizabeth Taylor, Dwayne "The Rock" Johnson, Florence Pugh

Personal Energy Number 2

Archetype: The Teacher

Sharing wisdom is your ultimate goal in life, and to do so, you will need to explore all the possible ways to gain the right knowledge and wisdom. When people around you have problems, you are the first to offer your advice and comfort. The women in your network and family will bring you the greatest support, as they are your teachers and mentors.

♦ Success Direction: Northeast

♦ Health Direction: West

♦ Relationship Direction: Northwest

♦ Wisdom Direction: Southwest

♦ Celebrities with this Energy Number: His Holiness the 14th Dalai Lama, Snoop Dogg, Blake Lively, Bella Hadid

Personal Energy Number 3

Archetype: The Bringer of Light

Through your music and dance, you bring life and light to people. For you, life is full of passion and change. Let go of all stress in your professional life. Friends are your important treasures and will always bring you good fortune. Family life will give you inspiration and wisdom.

♦ Success Direction: South

♦ Health Direction: North

♦ Relationship Direction: Southeast

♦ Wisdom Direction: East

♦ Celebrities with this Energy Number: Lizzo, Robin Williams, Kylie Jenner, Adele

Personal Energy Number 4

Archetype: The Manager

With a clear vision of the future, you start projects, planning and organizing every step until they are perfect. Nature is a source of happiness for your relationships with family and friends. You enjoy the sun. You must learn how to share your abundance with others.

- Success Direction: North

- Health Direction: South

- Relationship Direction: East

- Wisdom Direction: Southeast

- Celebrities with this Energy Number: Kobe Bryant, Winona Ryder, Jack Black, Kim Kardashian

Personal Energy Number 5 (Male)

Archetype: The Teacher
....

Sharing wisdom is your ultimate goal in life, and to do so, you will need to explore all possible ways to gain the right knowledge and wisdom. When people around you have problems, you are the first to offer your advice and comfort. The women in your network and family will bring you the greatest support as they are your teachers and mentors.

- Success Direction: Northeast

♦ Health Direction: West

♦ Relationship Direction: Northwest

♦ Wisdom Direction: Southwest

♦ Celebrities with this Energy Number: Drake, Tom Brady, Hugh Jackman, Robert Pattinson

Personal Energy Number 5 (Female)

Archetype: The Connector

You nurture others with your talents and gifts. You work best when you collaborate and team up with others. You need others to take care of your creativity, and communication is the bridge in your relationships. Meditating or praying is essential for your growth.

♦ Success Direction: Southwest

♦ Health Direction: Northwest

♦ Relationship Direction: West

♦ Wisdom Direction: Northeast

♦ Celebrities with this Energy Number: Dolly Parton, Cameron Diaz, Britney Spears, Beyoncé

Personal Energy Number 6

Archetype: The Creator
....

You are a creative thinker and innovator in both your professional and personal lives. New technologies are a passion of yours, and you love to have the latest gadgets. To you, women are goddesses and you relate better to women than to men. You are always ready to help others grow to be better human beings, and in your circle of friends your wisdom is appreciated.

- Success Direction: West

- Health Direction: Northeast

- Relationship Direction: Southwest

- Wisdom Direction: Northwest

- Celebrities with this Energy Number: Guy Fieri, Meryl Streep, Justin Bieber, Kamala Harris

Personal Energy Number 7

Archetype: The Advisor
....

Your focus is on the greater good for all. Your health is improved by nurturing yourself. In your relationships, you honor the talents of others and help those around you to progress to the next level. Children are a source of constant inspiration to you.

♦ Success Direction: Northwest

♦ Health Direction: Southwest

♦ Relationship Direction: Northeast

♦ Wisdom Direction: West

♦ Celebrities with this Energy Number: Tiger Woods, Gordon Ramsey, David Beckham, Billie Eilish

Personal Energy Number 8
Archetype: The Connector

You nurture others with your talents and gifts. You work best when you collaborate and team up with others. You need others to take care of your creativity, and communication is the bridge in your relationships. Meditating or praying is essential for your growth.

♦ Success Direction: Southwest

♦ Health Direction: Northwest

♦ Relationship Direction: West

- ♦ Wisdom Direction: Northeast

- ♦ Celebrities with this Energy Number: Will Smith, Arnold Schwarzenegger, Avril Lavigne, Ariana Grande

Personal Energy Number 9
Archetype: The Healer

You are open to new ideas, possibilities, and perspectives. Money can create stress for your health, so make sure your accounts are in order. Do not become a hermit. Enjoy the people around you. Music and dance will inspire you in your spiritual life.

- ♦ Success Direction: East

- ♦ Health Direction: Southeast

- ♦ Relationship Direction: North

- ♦ Wisdom Direction: South

- ♦ Celebrities with this Energy Number: Nicole Kidman, Jerry Seinfeld, Halsey, Ed Sheeran

When you've downloaded the Marie Diamond app, you'll have access to the Diamond Compass. With this compass, you'll be able to see the location of your Success Direction in blue, your Health Direction in green, your Relationship Direction in pink, and your Wisdom Direction in yellow. If you don't have access to the Marie Diamond app, you will need a physical compass to locate your Personal Directions. Make sure your compass has all eight directions displayed and is accurate to two degrees. Have a pen and a notepad to hand so that you can jot down your findings.

How Do I Use My Personal Energy Number?

There are two ways to use your Personal Energy Number. The first step is called "positioning," and the second step is called "activating." This chapter will talk about positioning.

To put it very simply, positioning refers to the arrangement of furniture (most importantly your bed and your desk) to ensure that it's facing one of your Personal Directions.

What's the Importance of Facing One of Your Personal Directions?

As you may remember from the introduction, Feng Shui allows your home to send out messages to the Universe and/or God. These messages contain information about what it is you want in your life, your goals, your dreams, and your ambitions.

Now, your Personal Directions are like a direct doorway straight to the Universe and/or God. Using these areas correctly will attract the things you want faster and more effectively.

With this in mind, here's a list of three things that you should aim to have facing toward one of your Personal Directions. While it would be perfect to have all three aligned with a Personal Direction, you should aim to have at least one of the following in place.

1. The Position of Your Front Door

The direction that your front door is facing should be in one of the four Personal Directions of the breadwinner of the home. To check the direction, stand in the door frame, facing out of your home toward the garden, the street, or the elevator in an apartment building, and hold a compass at heart level in front of you. This can be either the Diamond Compass on the Marie Diamond app or a physical one.

Write down the direction you're currently facing.

✎ ....

2. The Position of Your Bed

Your bed should be positioned so that when you go to sleep, the top of your head is pointing toward one of your Personal Directions. To check this direction, stand in the middle of the foot of the bed and look toward the headboard.

Write down the direction you're currently facing.

....

If this direction matches one of your four Personal Directions (while also following the power position rules discussed in the previous chapter)—perfect! You don't need to change anything.

If it doesn't match one of your four Personal Directions, use the compass to work out which direction you should move your bed to. Again, make sure that you're still following the power position rules discussed in the previous chapter.

You should find that you're able to move your bed so that it's facing at least one of your Personal Directions, although you may need to get a little creative with the layout of the room.

Write down the new direction you're facing.

....

3. The Position of Your Desk

The desk in your home office should be facing one of your four Personal Directions. To check this direction, sit behind your desk with the compass in the direction you're facing. Make sure that any electrical equipment on the desk is switched off (including computers, tablets, and lamps) so as not to interfere with the compass.

Write down the direction you're currently facing.

✎
....

If this direction matches one of your four Personal Directions (while also following the power position rules discussed in the previous chapter)—amazing! You don't need to change anything.

If it doesn't match one of your four Personal Directions, use the compass to work out which direction you should move your desk to. Again, make sure that you're still following the power position rules discussed in the previous chapter.

It should be easier to move your desk to face one of your Personal Directions since it's smaller than your bed, so you will have more options for where to place it.

Write down the new direction you're facing.

✎
....

Remember, you want to have as many of the above as possible facing one of your Personal Directions—and definitely at least one of them.

What Should I Do If I'm Not Able to Face Any of My Personal Directions?

In an ideal world, we'd all be able to move our beds, desks, and even doors to the directions that work best for us. In reality, things aren't always that simple. Whether it's a room with sloping ceilings, uneven lengths of walls, or built-in cabinets and closets, there are lots of practical obstacles that can prevent us from positioning things where we'd like to.

The beautiful thing about Feng Shui, though, is that it doesn't demand perfection—it's not an "all or nothing" approach. It just requires us to make the best of what we've got. So long as you have at least your front door, your bed, or your desk facing one of your Personal Directions, then you'll still be making the best use of the energy in your home.

What Should I Do If My Partner and I Have Different Personal Directions?

If you live with and share a bed with a partner, it can be tricky to position things to accommodate both people's Personal Directions.

Personal Energy Numbers can be divided into two categories: those belonging to West people and those belonging to East people.

East People	West People
Energy numbers: 1, 3, 4, 9	Energy numbers: 2, 5 (male), 5 (female), 6, 7, 8
Combinations of East, North, Southeast, and South	Combinations of West, Northwest, Southwest, and Northeast

East people will normally be able to find a common direction with other East people (same with West people with other West people). However, it can get difficult when, for example, you are a West person and your partner is an East person, because it means that you will have opposite Personal Directions. Don't worry, though, because there is a way to deal with this!

So, how do we get around this?

Well, as you will remember, each person needs at least one of the following facing one of their Personal Directions: the front door, their bed, or their desk. In the instance of opposite Personal Directions, if one of you has the front door facing one of their Personal Directions, you will need to make sure the bed is facing one of the Personal Directions of the other person.

For example, let's say Person A has a Personal Energy number of 6 and Person B has a Personal Energy number of 9. In their home, the door faces Southwest. This is one of the Personal Directions for Person A. To compensate, they move the bed so that it faces East, North, South, or Southeast, which is one of the Personal Directions for Person B. This way, they both have at least one item in the list facing one of their Personal Directions.

In the example shown below in Figure 1, due to the positioning of the bedroom door, the only option would be to move the bed so that it faces North. Moving it to face either East or South would mean that you wouldn't be able to have a clear view of the door without having to turn your head. Although Southeast would be another potential Personal Direction to use, there would be no room in this example because of the location of the door.

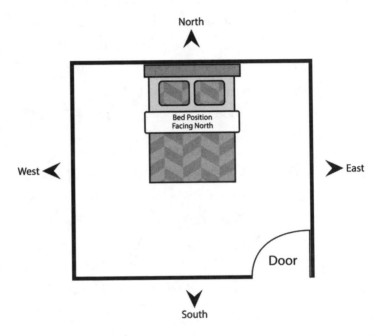

Figure 1: Placing the bed

Don't forget about each person's desk, too! Whether you both have a desk in the same room, or you have separate home offices, moving your desk to face one of your Personal Directions can be an easy way of ticking off another item on the list.

CHAPTER 7

Feng Shui for Success

As mentioned in the previous chapter, the second step in using your Personal Energy Number is called activating. This involves placing certain objects and images in your Personal Directions in order to attract different things. In this chapter, the focus will be on activating your Success Direction.

Since you should already know your Personal Energy Number by now, go to the Marie Diamond app and use the Diamond Compass to locate your Success Direction, or turn back to the table in Chapter 6. Remember, you should be standing in the center of the room when checking the compass points. The most important room to activate your Success Direction in will be your home office, but there will be things you can do to activate other areas in the house, too.

Once you've located your Success Direction, begin by getting rid of any unnecessary clutter in this area. Make sure everything is clean and organized and if you have a trash can placed here, move it to an area that isn't one of your four Personal Directions. As you can imagine, having trash in your Success Direction doesn't send out the best message to the Universe. If you've been wondering why you're having such a hard time trying to manifest your goals, it may be because you're literally throwing them away in the trash!

Now that you have some space cleared, place a table, bookcase, or a pin board here so you can display your crystals, photos, and other money-making accessories on it. If there's something in the way, such as a door or a built-in piece of furniture that means there isn't room for a table, consider putting up a shelf on the wall instead or hanging up a pin board. Whatever you use, make sure that it's elevated off the floor so that you're not looking down at it.

Activating Your Success with Your Front Door

As we've seen, the front door plays a very important role in Feng Shui, so we must make sure to include it in our activation for success. For your home, ensure that your front door is clean, free from clutter, and easily visible. Consider getting some solar powered lights in your front yard to help keep your door illuminated in the evening and during the darker months. For the front door of your office, have your company name and logo clearly visible. You want to make sure opportunities are able to find you at any given time.

If you have a welcome mat, be sure to replace it any time it gets a hole. Most importantly, your welcome mat shouldn't have your name or your company's name on it, for example: "The Smith Family" or "Bryce & Sons." Think about it: Do you want people coming into your home or office to trample all over your name with their dirty feet? It creates the symbolism of having people "walk all over you" so it's best to stick to a neutral, more basic message such as "welcome."

Activating Your Success with Images and Symbols

In your Success Direction, display photos of people you think are successful, either by hanging these on the walls or displaying them on the table you've already set out there. They can be photos of famous millionaires, or photos of innovators and entrepreneurs, for example. You should also display any of your diplomas, certificates, or degrees in orange frames as a way of celebrating all the success you've already had.

Also display objects that represent your business and how you currently make your money. These objects can include company logos displayed in a gold frame, important business contracts you've signed, any products that you've worked on (this can include anything from copies of books you've published, to the handmade items you sell on Etsy), or framed photos of you with important clients.

In your Success Direction, you can also set out fake awards, like an Oscar statue or a sports medal, which represent something you want to achieve. Engrave them with your name and the category type you wish to win; for example, a model of a Grammy with your name and "Best Pop Vocal Album" on it. Just like how we write our goals in the present tense as though we've already achieved them, these awards can be powerful tools for manifestation.

Outside your front door (either of your home or office), you can attract good fortune by placing a pair of items, one on either side of the door, such as a pair of lamps, a pair of round-leafed plants, or a pair of fu dogs.

❝ *I once visited the house of a man who seemed to be forever getting into accidents. In just a short amount of time, he'd broken his leg, his arm, and his wrist—all the results of separate incidents! While inspecting his home, I found that he had a statue of a man with no arms and no legs displayed in his Success Direction. Could it be that he was sending out a message to the Universe that he wanted to get rid of his limbs? Whatever the case, the statue was removed and his trips to the emergency room stopped.* **❞**

Activating Your Success with Colors

In Diamond Feng Shui, the colors for attracting success are royal blue, cobalt blue, orange, and peach. Royal blue represents power, cobalt blue represents empowerment, orange represents celebrations (for example, in anticipation of a promotion or the successful completion of a work project), and peach represents work satisfaction. In your Success Direction, add candles, tablecloths, and other soft furnishings and accessories in these colors.

Activating Your Success with Stationery

Additionally, you can also use the colors above to Feng Shui your stationery! When filing away your papers and documents, choose the following colors:

♦ royal blue folders for very important projects or for any projects where you feel you aren't being shown enough respect

♦ cobalt blue folders for projects that you're currently undertaking

♦ gold-colored folders for documents relating to money

♦ orange folders for documents relating to networking, business contacts, or HR matters. Also use to store any applications for awards or promotions.

♦ peach folders for projects that you want to find more joy in

♦ aqua blue folders for projects you need to do more research on

♦ yellow folders for future projects that you want to be a part of, or for any current projects that require a little extra inspiration

♦ violet folders for anything relating to spiritual matters or projects that require a little extra motivation

Label your folders with a gold marker on a white sticky label. Store them away in your filing cabinet, which should be kept in your Success Direction. Make sure these folders, or indeed any stationery, aren't kept on your desk when they're not in use. It's bad Feng Shui to have folders or stationery in front of you or within arm's reach, or to have them placed on the ground. Instead, you can keep them in a drawer hidden away or in a filing cabinet so they're not in sight.

Choose a gold notebook to use for writing down your success goals. Keep this notebook in your Success Direction when you're not writing in it. For an everyday brainstorming notebook, pick one in aqua blue. This will give you clarity in your ideas, push you to be proactive, and help you reach those genius "aha!" moments.

Similarly, pick out a special pen with a gold-colored barrel and only use it for writing in your gold notebook or for signing contracts. This sends out a message to the Universe that you respect your success enough not to sign your signature with any old ballpoint pen that's lying around. Carry it with you in your bag so that you're always prepared for any business opportunities that may come your way.

Activating Your Success with Furniture

Office furniture plays an important part in attracting success. Think about it: What would your first thoughts be if you were to walk into an office with shabby, broken furniture and you were given a chair to sit down on that had a wonky leg and torn stuffing? Not too good, I can imagine! You want to give off the impression that your workspace is a place of comfort and luxury. You don't need to spend a fortune, but it would definitely be worth investing a little extra money to ensure that your desk and office chair, at the very least, are the best they can be.

Avoid having a see-through glass or glass-top desk. While it may look hip, see-through furniture in Feng Shui can actually lead to financial deals and opportunities "falling through." Instead, a sturdy, wooden desk will be much better in helping you attract financial abundance. Pick one with strong legs and avoid one with a roll-top. Wood is an ideal material since it represents growth, whereas metal can magnify the electromagnetic fields of your computer equipment and be bad for your well-being.

As you can see in Figure 2, the desk has been positioned so that the person is sat facing the wall with the door to the office behind them. Their desk is too close to the door, which means there's no space for potential clients to sit, and there's a trash can located in their Success Direction. The desk itself and indeed the whole room seem to be littered with mess and clutter. This prevents the incoming flow of fresh, abundance-attracting energy, so the energy in the room may start to feel sluggish and stale.

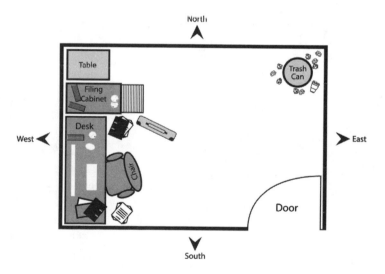

Figure 2: Bad office layout

As you can see in Figure 3, the desk is facing toward the door with a large enough space between the two. The chair is up against the wall and there are two chairs in front of the desk, a welcoming sign for potential clients. In this example, the person's Success Direction is in the Northeast, so a filing cabinet and a small table displaying work-related awards and products have been placed in this area.

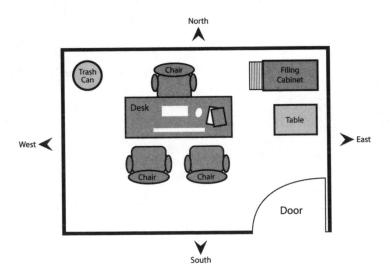

Figure 3: Good office layout

For your chair, avoid one with a low back, no armrests, no neck support, or with slats or holes in the back. It's important to have a chair that supports your back and neck correctly. When you have one that can do this, you'll find that not only are you less likely to experience aches and pains as a result of sitting awkwardly, but you'll also feel safer emotionally. When our back and neck are exposed, the "reptilian" part of our brain feels unsafe and is therefore more likely to push us to make decisions based on fear. However, when our back and neck are protected, we can make more careful, considered decisions based on logic, because we know those important body parts aren't in any immediate danger.

Investing in a chair with ample back and neck support is particularly important if you're unable to move your chair to face the door (for example, if you work in a cubicle or in an office with a fixed seating plan). Even if you have to pay for the chair out of your own pocket, it could be one of the most important things you do to boost your success.

It's key that the desk in your office is facing your Success Direction while also still facing the door. This may mean that you have to place your desk at a slight angle, but feel free to play around with the floor plan until you find something that suits you.

Activating Your Success with Scents

Using scents is a quick and easy way to boost the energy flow. For attracting success, look for room sprays, scented candles, or cleaning products containing white jasmine, ylang-ylang, or cinnamon.

Keep a scented candle on your desk and light it whenever you are working on an important project. You can also use essential oils to anoint your business files or filing cabinets to infuse their contents with good fortune.

Activating Your Success with Crystals

Emerald, citrine, or jade gemstones are all excellent crystals for attracting prosperity and financial success. You can place them in your Success Direction, or, as an alternative, emerald and jade can be placed in the Southeast and citrine can be placed in the Northwest. You can also use gemstone trees made from these crystals as a way to activate your success.

Whatever crystals you decide to use, make sure you're recharging them regularly so that they're always at their most effective (see Chapter 14 for information on how to do so).

Activating Your Success with Mirrors

In Feng Shui, mirrors are very powerful "doubling" tools, so you have to be very careful where you place them. If you want to attract more clients or customers into your office or place of business, hang up a mirror on one of the side walls next to the front door. This will have the effect of "doubling" the number of people coming in through the door.

However, avoid hanging one up directly in front of your desk since it may have the effect of "doubling" your workload and any work-related stress, particularly if it's a big mirror. Hanging a small mirror to the side of your desk is fine, though.

Activating Specific Business Success Goals

If you're looking to achieve a particular goal, here are a few more ways to activate your Success Direction.

If you're a company employee and are looking to receive a promotion, be sure to display:

♦ a photo of you with your boss or manager. Make sure that you're either both seated or standing together, as this sends out the message: "I am equal to that person."

- a logo of the company you work for

- your specific goal written down; for example: "I am working as an executive manager and enjoying all my newfound responsibilities"

- a business card either belonging to a person already in the role you want to be promoted to, or a card that you've mocked up with your name and desired role printed on it

- a photo of yourself in a royal blue frame

If you're looking to achieve a specific work goal as an employee at a company, be sure to display your goals written down and displayed in a cobalt blue frame.

If you're looking to achieve a specific goal as someone who is self-employed or who owns their own company, be sure to display:

- a logo of your business if applicable. You can also display the logos of any online marketplace service platforms you use for work.

- images of the products, books, or services you offer (this can be in the form of a marketing flier) displayed in golden frames. This is particularly important if you want to increase awareness or promote a new product or service.

If you're looking to get recognition in your field, be sure to display a photo of yourself displayed in an orange frame.

If you're looking to increase success in a multi-level marketing company, be sure to display:

♦ images of both your upper and down line

♦ photos of notable people who you admire from your upper line displayed in royal blue frames

How Else Can I Attract Success?

When signing a business contract, make sure you're sitting either facing your Success Direction or, if that's not possible, facing the door. If you have an important meeting at an external office, conference room, or at a coffee shop or restaurant, get there early and choose a seat that allows you to sit in the power position. At the very least, make sure that you're never sitting with your back to the door. Remember, the door can be in your peripheral view but you shouldn't have to turn your head to see it. If you're not happy with the choice of seating, ask a server if you're able to move to another table. The best table in this situation is one where you and your guest can both see the door.

In order to attract success while on the go, there are some essential items that you should always carry with you. Always have your gold pen and a notebook (ideally one with a blue cover) in your bag for any sudden bursts of inspiration. Carry your business cards in a gold-colored holder and have a separate orange holder to store the cards you collect from others.

When being introduced to other people, give a strong, firm handshake and use essential oils to anoint your wrists beforehand. Not only will this help you to activate your energy, it will leave a nice, pleasant smell. Use ylang-ylang to relax or lavender to help ease stress.

If you have a work phone or a work computer, pick your wallpaper wisely. It might be tempting to have a photo of a relaxing nature scene or a photo of your family, but these won't help put you in a mindset for work. Instead, change your wallpaper to something more work-oriented, such as your company logo or a team photo of you with your colleagues, or an inspirational business quote. When you sit down to make a call or write an email, you want your mind to be solely focused on the task at hand. Save the cute family shots or travel pictures for your leisure time!

> **66** *I once worked with a very famous music producer who was in a bit of a career slump. He was looking to make some changes to help kick-start his career and came to me for guidance. When he switched on his computer, I immediately noticed a problem—his wallpaper was a photo he'd taken while traveling through a desert. Although it was a very striking image, I told him, "Do you think that's the best image to have in the background while you work? The desert, with its droughts, dust, and tumbleweed?" Suddenly the penny dropped for him! The things we look at and have around us, even if we're not consciously aware of it, have a massive influence on what we manifest. He changed his wallpaper to a photo of him on stage receiving an award and, soon enough, his phone started ringing again.* **99**

CHAPTER 8

Feng Shui for Money

In this chapter, we'll be once again be activating your Success Direction, but this time with a particular focus on attracting more money.

There are three main objectives in money activation. The first is to let the Universe know exactly what it is that you wish to attract; the second is to give yourself a visual reminder as motivation to keep your eyes on the prize; and the third is to help you develop a healthy respect for money. You want to send out the message that you understand the power that money can bring, and that you're capable of handling it. You're not stuffing bank statements in the bottom of a messy desk drawer or letting your loose change gather dust in your bag— you're letting that Universe know that you're ready to receive!

Activating Your Money with Your Front Door

As mentioned in the previous chapter, the doors of your home play an important role in Feng Shui. In relation to money, your front door is connected to your career and active income while your back door is related to passive income (for example, royalties). In order to increase either one of these things, it's important to keep the areas around your doors clean, clear, and free from clutter.

Activating Your Money with Images and Symbols

In your Success Direction, either by hanging them on the walls or placing them on the table you've already set out there, display artwork or images that depict gently flowing water, such as a river or stream. Water is the most important element in terms of attracting money, so these will be very powerful images to have. For more information on how to use water in Feng Shui, turn to Chapter 16.

Similarly, you can display images of flowers coming into bloom or lush nature scenes. Anything that represents growth or blossoming will have a positive effect on your cash flow.

You can also display images that represent abundance to you. This can include anything from high-end designer fashion campaigns to paintings of diamonds and jewels—whatever most resonates with you. Hanging up a photo of yourself in a gold-colored photo frame is another way to attract abundance.

> **Look at what hangs on the wall that you face when you're sitting at your desk. If there's nothing hanging up, display something that inspires you that you can look at while you work.**

On the other hand, there are some images that you should avoid displaying since they'll have the complete opposite effect. Winter scenes, although beautiful, represent struggle and hardship. If you have any images of mountains, make sure they're not snowcapped. Similarly, desert scenes represent drought, so avoid displaying anything to do with sand, cacti, or barren environments.

If you like artwork with geometric prints, avoid those with a lot of sharp or pointed edges. In Feng Shui, the flow of energy can get "stuck" on anything too sharp or pointed, so go for images with curved, rounded patterns to keep the flow of energy (and money!) moving.

Money frogs have traditionally been used to bring good luck into the home. A money frog is a three-legged frog with a gold coin in its mouth. Now, it may be tempting to place this little money-magnet in every single room. However, you only actually need to place one diagonally across from your front door (never directly across from it). Position the frog on the ground so that it's facing toward the door (either the front door of your house or the door to your office or workspace) so that money flows in, rather than out. The money frog is a powerful symbol in Feng Shui, so make sure that you're dusting it regularly, you're keeping the surrounding area clean, and that you replace it should it ever get damaged or broken.

Place a gold bowl in the Southeast or Northwest area of your entrance area or living room (not in the kitchen) that will be used specifically for holding loose change. By having a special place to store your coins and small bills, you're showing the Universe that you respect money enough to save it, no matter how small the amount. Make it a habit that whenever you come home, you place any loose change in it that you find in your pockets, coat, or handbag.

In your Success Direction, you can set out books about money, investing, trading, or cryptocurrency. You can also set out biographies about successful business people or wealthy people that you admire.

> Avoid having large images or statues of fierce animals like tigers and lions around you. Since the presence of these animals is quite threatening, you may find yourself criticized and "attacked" over the value of your work.

Activating Your Money with Colors

In Diamond Feng Shui, the colors for attracting money are gold and silver. Gold represents abundance, and silver represents magnificence. In your Success Direction, add candles, tablecloths, and other soft furnishings and accessories in these colors. You can also add an extra "oomph!" to any images or photos you display by putting them in gold or silver photo frames.

Activating Your Money with Furniture

In your office, place a small filing cabinet in your Success Direction to file away your financial records and bank statements. Make sure that your papers have been well organized and filed away in the appropriate color folders (refer back to the previous chapter for a breakdown of Feng Shui stationery). From a practical standpoint, a well-organized filing system will do wonders for giving you a clear picture of your financial situation, but it's also another thing you can do to show the Universe that you treat money seriously. You should also place any equipment you use to take payment (such as electronic card readers) in this filing cabinet.

In your living or dining room, your dining table has an effect on your cash flow. Make sure that you always keep it clean and set out a vase of fresh or silk flowers on top (avoid dried flowers, though, because their lack of life force makes the surrounding energy flow stagnant). You can also set out a bowl of orange, clementines, or red apples. Ensure this bowl is always kept full as it represents your treasures remaining forever bountiful!

Activating Your Money with Scents

Using scents is a quick and easy way to boost the energy flow. For attracting money, look for room sprays, scented candles, or cleaning products containing white jasmine, sandalwood, ylang-ylang, peppermint, or eucalyptus essential oil.

Keep a scented candle on your desk and light it whenever you are working on an important project. You can also use essential oils to anoint your bank files or filing cabinet to infuse its contents with good fortune.

Activating Your Money with Crystals

Pyrite, jade, emerald, citrine, tiger's eye, and white quartz gemstones are all excellent crystals for attracting prosperity. You can also use gemstone trees made from these particular crystals as a way to activate your financial success.

Place them in your Success Direction and make sure you're recharging them regularly so that they're always at their most effective (see Chapter 14 for information on how to do so).

Activating Your Money with Mirrors

When used correctly, mirrors can be a very effective money-attracting tool in Feng Shui. Since they have a "doubling" effect, you can use them to double your luck and abundance, but if used incorrectly, they can just as easily double your bad luck! In your living room, hang up a mirror on the longest wall opposite your dining table so that the vase of flowers or fruit bowl you've set out is reflected in the mirror.

In your bathroom, however, make sure any mirror you have out doesn't face the toilet since this will cause you to lose money very quickly. Ideally, you wouldn't have a toilet directly above your front door, but if you do, you can neutralize this by securing a mirror to the ceiling, mirror-side facing up, under where the toilet is located. This will direct all that negative energy flow back up.

Activating Specific Money Success Goals

In addition to activating your Success Direction, there are some other general directions that you may wish to activate in order to achieve specific money-related goals.

If you're looking to increase your cash flow in relation to your career (for example, you want a pay rise or you're a writer wishing to sell more books), you can activate the North direction of your home office by displaying:

◆ images of gently flowing, moving water. It's very important that the water doesn't look still, as in the case of a pond. Similarly, avoid any images that feature boats that look like they've anchored—you want everything in the image to look as if there's some movement behind it.

◆ a water fountain

◆ blue items

◆ pyrite and white quartz

If you're looking to attract more income streams, you can activate your Success Direction by displaying:

♦ a Chinese pagoda. You can also place one behind you in order to increase your passive income.

♦ a book by or an image of a successful and wealthy entrepreneur, such as Oprah Winfrey or Richard Branson

If you're looking to attract better long-term investments (for example, real estate opportunities), you can activate the Northwest direction of your home office by displaying:

♦ a bowl of coins. If you have business dealings with associates or companies based in a specific country, include some coins from their currency too.

♦ a round, white crystal (such as white quartz) or citrine

If you're looking to increase your cryptocurrency wallet, you can activate the West direction of your home office by displaying:

♦ silver items

♦ citrine

If you're looking to attract better deals or opportunities in relation to stocks, bonds, or savings, you can activate the Southeast direction of your home office by displaying:

♦ a water fountain

♦ a bamboo plant or a blooming orchid

♦ gold items

♦ jade, emerald or pyrite

> **Are you looking for new career opportunities? Let go of the past by storing all your old business papers or contracts either digitally or in a box that you can put into storage.**

How Else Can I Attract Money?

Since activation is all about showing your intentions to the Universe, there are several things you can do to show the Universe that you wish to attract money. Anytime you get a notification that someone has paid you (either from an online sale, a settled invoice, or simply your monthly paycheck), take a moment to send a message of gratitude to that person. You don't literally have to send them a message (although that might be thoughtful!); just close your eyes, keep their name in your mind, and say a quiet message of thanks to that person for what they've given you. Similarly, anytime you have to pay out money to someone, be grateful that the service they've provided you with is helping you to grow your own abundance.

You can go one step further and make sure that when you're checking your bank balance on your phone or making an online payment, you're facing toward your Success Direction. If that isn't always possible, make sure that you're at least facing the door so that you're making yourself available to the incoming flow of abundant energy and that you're not cutting yourself off from it.

> **Wear something blue or gold, such as a blue suit or a gold-colored watch, whenever you have a business meeting. Your power will shine through!**

CHAPTER 9

Feng Shui for Health

This chapter will focus on activating your Health Direction in order to attract good physical and mental health, vitality, and longevity.

Think back to the origins of Feng Shui and how it was used primarily by Chinese emperors and noble people in power. They wanted to ensure that they lived long, healthy lives in order to maximize their reign. They also wished to guarantee that they had strong, healthy children who could then hand on the family legacy. It was longevity that was originally the main focus of Feng Shui, not success or money.

Nowadays, good health means more than just living a long time and having children. It can mean improving your quality of living, looking after your mental health, and making the time for self-care. By activating your Health Direction in your office or workspace (where you are during the day) and your bedroom (where you are during the night), you'll be able to use the energy flow of your home to attract good health to you and those you live with.

Activating Your Health with Images and Symbols

In your Health Direction in both your office and bedroom, you can place books relating to medicine or healthy living (for example, books about yoga, a healthy recipe book, or a medical journal), your vitamins and supplements, and any business cards from your doctor, health practitioners, or alternative medicine therapists.

Activating Your Health with Houseplants

Green, leafy plants are vital in bringing that fresh, living energy into a space. To make the most of this life force, place large plants in the East of your living room or office, medium-sized plants in the South, and smaller plants in the Southeast. For more information on the Feng Shui benefits of houseplants and flowers, turn to Chapter 15.

Activating Your Health with Candles

Candles are similarly vital because fire represents longevity, so place them in any direction around your living room, office, and bedroom. Fireplaces can attract good health, but it depends on what direction they're located. Ideally, they would be located in the South, Southwest, Center or Northeast areas of the house. If the fireplace is in the Northwest, place blue objects around it and if it's in the East, place green objects around it.

Activating Your Health with Colors

In Diamond Feng Shui, the colors for attracting health are emerald green, white, and purple. In your Health Direction, add candles, tablecloths, and other soft furnishings and accessories in these colors.

In general, avoid using too many blues, greens, or reds in any room, particularly in the bedroom. "Too much" refers to having carpets, wall colors, curtains, and soft furnishings all in the same color—a complete visual overload! Too much blue can lead to emotional issues, such as feelings of depression or loneliness. Too much green can cause sleep issues, because, surrounded by so much green, our brain can think that we're in nature, so it stays on high alert in case of predators or danger. Too much red can cause extreme reactions and heightened emotions, since red is a color of passion.

The best color palettes to use for each room are earth tones: beiges, browns, peaches, yellows, and soft pinks. These colors are soothing for the mind and help promote a peaceful emotional state.

Avoiding Poison Arrows

If you have a bedroom with beams, especially if there's one directly over your head while you sleep, this is known in Feng Shui as a "poison arrow" and can lead to health issues. To neutralize it, paint it or cover it with material in the same color as the ceiling so that it blends in.

Activating Your Health with Crystals

Jade, emerald, and amethyst gemstones are all excellent crystals for attracting good health. You can use gemstone trees made from these particular crystals too.

Place them in your Health Direction and make sure you're recharging them regularly so that they're always at their most effective (see Chapter 14 for information on how to do so).

Avoiding Mirrors in Your Bedroom

Sleeping in your bedroom with a mirror (or any reflective surface, like a TV screen) across from you can "double" any health issues you face. It can also lead to bad dreams and a restless night. As a solution, cover these mirrors or surfaces with a scarf or a fold-out screen while you sleep.

Activating Specific Health Goals

In addition to activating your Health Direction, there are some general directions that you may wish to activate in order to achieve specific health-related goals.

To help with the health of everyone in your home, activate the East with:

♦ plants with rounded leaves

♦ photos of people in your family who lived long, healthy lives

♦ a picture of your family tree

♦ emerald green items, such as candles or cushions

To help with female health issues, activate the Southwest with a rose quartz crystal.

To help with male health issues, activate the Northwest with a white quartz crystal.

To help with children's health issues, activate the West with photos of your children playing and being joyful.

To help with mental health issues, activate the Northeast with an amethyst crystal.

To help with any general health issues, activate the Center of the home. If there is a kitchen or bathroom in the center of the home, this can disrupt the balance of energies, so neutralize it by placing orange colors in those rooms (for example, paint the walls orange or include orange hand towels or rugs). It's also important not to have any clutter or trash cans placed in the Southwest, Northwest, West and Northeast directions of your living room.

Make a habit of emptying trash and garbage cans every night so that you're able to start each new day with fresh energy in your home.

Your Feng Shui First Aid Kit

In much the same way that a first aid kit contains things you might need in an emergency, like bandages, aspirin, or antiseptic wipes, your Feng Shui first aid kit should contain your must-have supplies, whatever the situation!

A Lavender Candle

Lavender is perfect for purifying the air and calming the energy around you. Whenever you feel like you need to relax or you need to cleanse the air around you, burning a lavender candle is a quick and easy fix.

A White Quartz Crystal

If you're only able to buy one crystal, this would be the one to invest in! A crystal with a "can-do" attitude, it has tremendous healing properties, protects against negative energy, and works to restore the balance of energy in a home.

A Bottle of Lavender Air Mist

As noted in Chapter 4, lavender air mist is great for freshening the energy of any room or area that feels stuffy or stale. It's also useful for times when you don't have easy access to a candle, such as when you're staying in a hotel and you want to quickly purify the space.

Incense Sticks

Incense is a great way not only to freshen the energy in the home, but to add the harmonizing element of air to a room. While incense is available in a wide range of wonderful scents, a classic nag champa always works well.

CHAPTER 10

Feng Shui for Romantic Relationships

This chapter will focus on activating your Relationship Direction, specifically to attract a new romantic relationship or to help maintain your existing romantic relationship.

In today's busy world, it can be difficult to find the time to make passion and romance a priority. It might be the case that you're looking to rekindle the "spark" in your long-term relationship, improve your communication skills with each other, or just for extra ways to enhance your connection together. It could also be the case that you're single and need some extra help to stop falling for the wrong people and to finally find your Prince (or Princess) Charming. Whatever you're looking for, Feng Shui is here to help!

Activating Your Relationships with Images, Photos, and Symbols

Take a look at the paintings, photos, and artwork you have hanging up in your bedroom at the moment. The first step is to take down anything that features people by themselves and replace them with images of couples embracing each other or dancing. If you're already in a relationship, you can also hang up your wedding photo or any photo of you and your partner looking particularly in love, displayed in a cherry-red frame.

If you want to add a splash of passion to your relationship, you can even display artwork featuring nudes or of couples kissing in your Relationship Direction. Displaying these images in a red photo frame is another way to add an extra "oomph!" to your love life.

Then remove any images that feature water. This can mean pictures of rivers, lakes, waterfalls, or beaches. In Feng Shui, water can represent peace and tranquility, but it can also "dampen" passion. Replace them with those that feature fire elements, such as of a couple sitting in front of a roaring fire, or watching colorful fireworks together. If you find that you and your partner are fighting a lot, it might mean that the artwork on display has too much chaotic energy. If that's the case, choose some more calming imagery of beautiful landscapes in bloom instead.

Lastly, turn your attention to the wall above the headboard of your bed. Pick a photo or image that best represents what it is you're looking to attract in a relationship—big romantic gestures? Comfort and cuddles? Passion and adventure? Whatever it is that most resonates with you and what you want, hang it up above your bed.

> ❝ A client of mine came to me once because she was tired of being so unlucky in love. While she enjoyed dating and had no problem meeting men, problems always came up whenever she invited them over to her house. No matter how well the date went, neither she nor her date ever wanted to "take things up to the bedroom," so to speak. The desire for intimacy was nonexistent, even if there had been sparks of passion there before. She was really upset, even going so far as to wonder if there was something medically wrong with her!
>
> I took a look at her home and immediately found the problem. Displayed all the way up from the stairs to her bedroom were biblical

images of Jesus and his crucifixion. The last image, of Jesus nailed to the cross, was directly outside her bedroom. No wonder she was having difficulties: Her home was sending out the message that bringing a man up to her bedroom would be like sending him off to his death! I told her if she were to immediately remove the images, she'd notice a drastic improvement. Sure enough, she came to me some months later to say that she'd started a relationship with a man who she was finally able to bring all the way up to her bedroom.

With respect to symbols and objects, try to display everything in your Relationship Direction in pairs (such as two red candles placed together, or two love heart ornaments) since this will help to ensure your relationship remains balanced and harmonious. You can also set out books about famous lovers throughout history or romantic works of fiction. If you have any love letters written to you by your current partner, display those proudly on a pin board in your Relationship Direction too!

Most importantly, though, remove any items from your Relationship Direction that remind you of past relationships. This can include any gifts given to you by an ex, any photos taken by an ex, or anything you bought together. This doesn't mean you have to get rid of them altogether, but keeping them in this area can cause friction in your current relationship or make it hard for you to move on to a new relationship.

Likewise, remove anything from your Relationship Direction relating to work (including work laptops), any sort of clutter, or anything that you don't think represents romance or passion!

If you and your partner have different Personal Energy Numbers, and therefore different Relationship Directions, it's perfectly fine to activate both of your Relationship Directions in your bedroom. This can be as simple as one partner displaying their wedding photo in their Relationship Direction, and the other partner displaying a vase of beautiful silk red roses in theirs.

If you have different Personal Energy Numbers and you're unsure how to position your bed properly, turn back to Chapter 6 where there is information on how to deal with this.

Feng Shui Your Life

Activating Your Relationships with Colors

In Diamond Feng Shui, the colors for attracting good romantic relationships are rose, peach, and orange. In your Relationship Direction, add these colors in the form of candles or romantically inspired artwork.

Activating Your Relationships with Crystals

Rose quartz is an excellent crystal for attracting and improving romantic relationships. You can also use gemstone trees made from this particular crystal. As a rule, make sure that you set out your rose quartz crystals in pairs. Better yet, see if you can find a rose quartz in the shape of a heart.

Place these crystals in your Relationship Direction and make sure you're recharging them regularly to ensure they're always at their most effective (see Chapter 14 for information on how to do so).

Activating Your Relationships with Flowers

As a quick note, while flowers are an excellent thing to use when activating your Relationship Direction, it is important that you only use fake flowers (silk flowers

♦ 100 ♦

are a good, high-quality option) or images of flowers in the bedroom. Real flowers come with a lot of life force, which can be too intense for the bedroom, a room that's primarily used for sleep! To help keep the energy calm and tranquil, save the bouquets of fresh flowers for the living room instead.

Red roses have long been associated with love and romance, making them an excellent thing to add to your Relationship Direction. This can be in the form of silk roses, or a piece of beautiful artwork featuring red roses. Rose-scented candles and air fresheners are also a great way to add the essence of rose to your bedroom, transforming it into a sweet-smelling space that's ready for romance!

If you're a single woman and looking for a steady romantic relationship, place a bouquet of peonies in your Relationship Direction. They can be made of silk or you can just display an image that depicts peonies. Once you've managed to attract the relationship you're looking for, be sure to pass on the peonies to one of your single friends. If you're a single man, you can do the exact same thing using a bamboo plant instead.

When using flowers, it's also very important not to use dried flowers. When it comes to romance and relationships, dried flowers symbolize death and decay— not exactly the things that great love stories are made of!

Activating Specific Relationship Goals

In addition to activating your own Relationship Direction, there are also some general directions that you may wish to activate in order to achieve specific relationship-related goals.

If you're having trouble moving on from a past relationship:

♦ Burn a violet candle in the Southeast corner of your bedroom while you gather up everything that reminds you of your ex. Then, wrap up the items in violet tissue paper before placing them in a box. You can either dispose of this box, or hide it safely away in a cupboard or closet.

♦ Declutter the Southwest area of your bedroom, letting go of any clothes, letters, or photos that remind you of them. Delete any emails or text messages from them.

♦ Let go of any artwork or other items that you bought together. Sell them or give them to charity.

If you would like to improve communication with your partner:

♦ Display a candle or object in aqua blue in the North corner of your bedroom.

♦ If you wish to heal your communication, display a candle or object in emerald green in the East corner of your bedroom.

If you're having trouble attracting a new partner:

♦ Make sure that there's room for a bedside table at each side of your bed, ready for your new partner. Likewise, make sure there's always a pillow on the bed ready for them.

♦ Set out fresh, clean towels in the bathroom for your new partner (make sure not to use them yourself!) and create some room in the bathroom cabinet so that there's space ready for them. You can take it another step further and leave out a clean toothbrush and a fresh bar of soap.

◆ When you sit down for dinner at your dining table, always set an extra place even if you're eating alone.

◆ All these things will help send a clear message to the Universe that you're ready for a new romance and that you've made the effort to make some extra room.

> Remove all paintings and statues that feature single people or animals as they may subconsciously be keeping you single and alone.

CHAPTER 11

Feng Shui for Professional Relationships

This chapter will focus on activating your Relationship Direction specifically to improve any professional relationships you have. This can include the relationships you have with any colleagues, your manager, supervisor, or boss. It also relates to networking and the relationships you have with your clients and customers.

Having good relationships with those you work with is a key part of being successful. After all, a co-worker who's always ready with a smile and a word of encouragement will get a lot farther ahead than someone who struggles to be a team player. Maintaining good professional relationships, especially with your clients, will do wonders for boosting your reputation and earning you respect in your industry.

When you activate the Relationship Direction of your office, you'll be able to promote teamwork and a sense of "belonging" amongst your co-workers, boost your confidence when networking, and make positive, effective connections with your clients and customers.

Activating Your Relationships with Images, Photos, and Symbols

If you work as an employee, display photos of yourself with your co-workers (including your managers or bosses) in the Relationship Direction of your office. If you have any photos taken during important work presentations, award ceremonies, or even company socials, display these too. Display any beautifully illustrated inspirational quotes about teamwork or the power of collaboration. Not only will they give you a boost of motivation when you look at them, but they'll work to manifest a feeling of "togetherness" in your team.

If you're a CEO or manager, you should still display photos of yourself with your team in the Relationship Direction of your office. This will remind you of the valuable work that they do in order to make your business vision a reality. Display photos of CEOs or managers that you admire, along with any quotes that inspire you to be a better leader.

If you work with clients or customers, try to have something in your Relationship Direction to represent them too. Are most of your clients online from all across the world, or are they specific to a certain city or country? Display an image that represents this—it can be a country flag or something that symbolizes the industry or any club or social group your clients might be associated with. If your clients are located all across the world, or if you're looking to expand your business worldwide, place a globe in this area too.

If you've ever received a good review from a customer (maybe an online review) or an award or certificate related to teamwork, cooperation, or community spirit at work, display this in your Relationship Direction. You can also display any goals you might have relating to your professional relationships, such as "I am widely known for my amazing customer service skills," or "Customers frequently tell me that they love working on projects with me."

If you want to try to increase the number of clients or customers you have, hang up a mirror to the side of the front door to your office. This way, you'll be "doubling" the number of customers walking through the door.

Activating Team Spirit with Furniture

If you work with others in an office, make sure that your desks are arranged in such a way that everyone is facing each other. Feelings of conflict or exclusion can start to fester when team members are literally working "behind other people's backs." Having people sit side by side is a much better way to keep the energy in the office harmonious and calm.

Having enough space in front of your desk for a chair or two for any potential customers to sit at will do wonders for attracting new clientele. You can even leave out reading material or complementary refreshments for your guests, so that they feel relaxed and pampered each time they come to your office.

Activating Your Relationships with Colors

In Diamond Feng Shui, fuchsia is the color for encouraging collaborations and enhancing teamwork. In your Relationship Direction, add candles or photo frames in this color. You can also add this color to any stationery you use for team projects, such as folders, binders, or sticky notes.

Activating Your Relationships with Crystals

Rose quartz is an excellent crystal for attracting and improving professional relationships. You can use gemstone trees made from this particular crystal too.

Place them in your Relationship Direction and make sure you're recharging them regularly to ensure they're always at their most effective (see Chapter 14 for information on how to do so).

Activating Specific Relationship Goals

In addition to activating your own Relationship Direction, there are some general directions that you may wish to activate in order to achieve specific relationship goals.

If you'd like to be able to collaborate better with your colleagues or business partners, place the following in the Southwest area of your office:

♦ a team photo

♦ a ceramic friendship circle

- copies of any business contracts or letters of collaboration

- any fuchsia-colored objects

If you want to be able to collaborate better with your manager, supervisor, mentor, or boss, place the following in the Northwest area of your office:

- a photo of you and them, either standing next to each other or both seated. Avoid any photos where one of you is standing and the other is seated as this can symbolize inequality.

- their business card with your business card attached to it

- fuchsia-colored objects

By making these changes, you will send a clear message to the Universe that you value your professional relationships, both with the people you work with and with those you work for. Making the changes shows that you have a healthy respect for teamwork and—with dedication like that—who knows what exciting opportunities for collaboration will come your way?

CHAPTER 12

Feng Shui for Family Relationships

This chapter will focus on activating your Relationship Direction specifically to help improve your family relationships. This can include any family members you share a home with, but also cousins, uncles, aunts, and grandparents who may live farther away.

The relationships we have with our families are often amongst the most important we can have, but that doesn't mean they might not drive us crazy sometimes! During your childhood, I'm sure there were moments when you and your parents didn't quite see eye to eye and if you have children of your own now, I'm sure there are times where you're absolutely convinced that you know best.

Activating the Relationship Direction in your living room will help to keep the energy flow in your home peaceful, loving, and harmonious—all essential things for keeping the whole family happy!

Activating Your Relationships with Images, Photos, and Symbols

In the Relationship Direction of your living room, display photos of yourself with your family members. Pick photos where you all seem to be happy and smiling and try to update these as often as possible. Include photos of yourself with your partner, your children, your siblings, your own parents, and any aunts, uncles, or grandparents. If you have a family crest or a copy of your family tree, it would also be good to display that in this area.

It's a great idea to hang up a family photo in the entrance area of your home. This way, your family will be acting as a united force, welcoming everyone who enters. However, two rooms where you should definitely avoid displaying any family photos are the bathroom and the kitchen. Parents should also avoid displaying any photos of their children in their master bedroom, as these can put a dampener on the room's romantic energy! On the other hand, displaying a photo of yourself and your partner in your child's Relationship Direction in their bedroom is an effective way to help children be more respectful and it also acts as a reminder of your love for them.

If you have any treasured family heirlooms or gifts given to you by a relative, display them in your Relationship Direction in your living room or bedroom. Honor these objects by making sure they're either cleaned or dusted regularly.

Activating Your Relationships with Colors

In Diamond Feng Shui, the colors for improving your family relationships are peach and orange. These two colors represent joy, harmony, and happiness, and are great ways to help boost the mood in your home.

In the Relationship Direction in your living room, add candles, tablecloths, and other soft furnishings and accessories in these colors. Adding peach-colored cushions to your sofa in the living room in particular is a quick and easy way to encourage open, interesting, and engaging conversations between those who sit there.

> The color of compassion is saffron yellow, so if you're having trouble seeing eye to eye with your family or you feel yourself being extra judgmental, try to add more saffron-colored accessories to the living room.

Activating Your Relationships with Crystals

White quartz crystal, rose quartz, and amethyst are all excellent crystals for attracting and improving family relationships. You can also use gemstone trees made from these particular crystals.

Place them in your Relationship Direction and make sure you're recharging them regularly to ensure they're always at their most effective (see Chapter 14 for information on how to do so).

Activating Specific Relationship Goals

In addition to activating your own Relationship Direction, there are some general directions that you may wish to activate in order to achieve specific relationship-related goals.

If, for example, you would like to make amends with any parents or siblings you've fallen out with, display the following in the East direction:

♦ a bouquet of fresh flowers in your living room or a bamboo plant

♦ a photo of you with that person that was taken during a happy time for you both, like a Christmas or a birthday celebration. This photo doesn't have to be recent; it can be from when you were younger or even a child.

If you need to have a difficult conversation with your children or partner (perhaps about missed curfews, forgotten chores, or trying to resolve an argument), display a sweet-smelling vanilla candle in the West direction if the conversation is with your children, or the Southwest direction if the conversation is with your partner. Light it five minutes before you call them in for the conversation. By that time, the air will smell sweet and the energy in the room will seem calmer.

Incorporating all these items into your living room or family space will help promote happy, harmonious relationships within your home.

CHAPTER 13

Feng Shui for Wisdom

This chapter will focus on activating your Wisdom Direction. Now, being "wise" can mean a lot of different things to a lot of different people. For some, it might mean focusing on their studies, having a degree, being an expert in their career field, or maybe even just reading a lot of books! For others, being wise can mean being devoted to their religion or spiritual journey. Before you begin activating this Direction, it's a good idea to sit down and think about what wisdom means to you. How do you connect with your wisdom? How did you come to understand your place in the world? Did it come from books and education, creativity, intuition, God, the Universe, saints, masters, or angels?

This is also a good time to offer a reminder that Feng Shui is not a religion but an energy system. However, it can be a useful tool to help you deepen the connection you have with your religion or your spirituality. By activating your Wisdom Direction, you're creating a special, dedicated place in your home that honors your religious and spiritual practices.

Activating Your Wisdom with Images, Photos, and Symbols

In the Wisdom Direction in your office and bedroom, you can place books relating to your chosen topics of study, biographies of people who inspire you, and books that you want to read to help you learn new things. Your Wisdom Direction is an excellent place for a bookcase in your bedroom or office so that you can store your books in a neat and organized way.

If you're a student, hang up a pin board in your Wisdom Direction to display your class timetable, a map of your school campus, or any other class materials. You can also hang up any educational certificates you've earned, such as diplomas, degrees, or awards from school. The Wisdom Direction is a particularly important direction for students, so be sure to activate it even if it just involves hanging up a pin board in your dorm room.

If you're religious or have a spiritual practice of any sort, your Wisdom Direction is the perfect place to display anything related to this, including religious and spiritual texts, books and biographies about important leaders or people from your spiritual path, statues, candles, and even an altar if you wish. Dedicate this space as your special place for prayer and for continuing your spiritual journey; anytime you feel lost and you're looking for answers, you can come to this space to reconnect with your inner wisdom. Facing toward your Wisdom Direction while you pray or meditate will also help to deepen your spiritual connection. If you don't have room in your Wisdom Direction for an altar, you can place it in the Northeast area of the room instead.

Since wisdom is linked to the earth element, you can activate this area with things that represent earth, such as crystals and images of mountains. However, make sure that the mountain in the photo isn't snowcapped since this can lead to you "freezing" your progress during your wisdom journey!

Activating Your Wisdom with Colors

In Diamond Feng Shui, the colors for wisdom are yellow, saffron yellow, purple, and aqua blue. In your Wisdom Direction, add candles, tablecloths, and other soft furnishings and accessories in these colors.

♦ 119 ♦

For students who need a little extra help in concentrating, iris blue is an excellent color for improving focus. Using notebooks with an iris blue-colored cover or incorporating this color into study notes can be a quick and easy way to prevent any pre-exam procrastination!

> Yellow is the color of sunlight and your intuition is the sunlight trapped within the prison of your ego. Place this color in the Northeast of your living room so that everyone living with you can attract wisdom and intuition.

Activating Your Wisdom with Scents

To help attract wisdom or deepen your spiritual or religious connections, look for room sprays, scented candles, or cleaning products containing frankincense, ylang-ylang, myrrh, or nag champa essential oils.

Keep a scented candle in your Wisdom Direction and light it anytime you're reading, studying, praying, or meditating.

Activating Your Wisdom with Crystals

Amethyst is a gemstone associated with wisdom and spirituality, so it's a very good one to have around. To help improve your intuition and bring clarity into your life, white quartz crystal is also very effective. You can use gemstone trees made from these particular crystals, too.

Place them in your Wisdom Direction and make sure you're recharging them regularly to ensure they're always at their most effective (see Chapter 14 for information on how to do so).

Activating Specific Wisdom Goals

In addition to activating your own Wisdom Direction, there are other things you can do to help you achieve specific wisdom-related goals.

To feel better connected with your intuition, display the following in your Wisdom Direction:

◆ a yellow candle

◆ a sheet of paper with a question written on it that you want help finding the answer to. You can place this paper underneath the yellow candle or near it—just make sure it's not in danger of catching alight!

◆ an amethyst

To help improve your school grades and become better focused, display the following in your Wisdom Direction:

♦ an image of the school you currently attend, or one that you'd like to attend in future

♦ a white quartz crystal

To help avoid writer's block while you write a book, display the following in your Wisdom Direction:

♦ a print-out of the book's front cover, even if it's just a draft or a mock-up

♦ information about the book or a short description

By making these adjustments, you should be able to strengthen your spiritual or religious connections, and also improve your educational pursuits. They will help to send the message to the Universe that you take your role as student of this world seriously, and that you're ready to receive wisdom whenever it comes.

CHAPTER 14

Activate Your Feng Shui with Crystals

Crystals play a very important role in Feng Shui. Both help to regulate the energy of a room, either by enhancing the flow of positive energy (Feng Shui) or by giving out positive energy and absorbing any negative energy (crystals).

Used for centuries for their healing powers, it's believed that crystals give out energy that can help increase the energy levels in our own bodies. This in turn can make us feel happier, healthier, and more positive. Not only that, but when they're put in the right place in your home, they can help activate that area, making it quicker and easier for you to attract whatever it is you're looking for!

How Do I Choose the Right Crystal?

Each crystal carries with it different properties. Some have healing properties, some can improve clarity and attract good luck, and some absorb negative emotions. Determining which crystal is best for you depends entirely on what it is that you need help with.

As a guide, here is a list of some of the most popular crystals, their properties, and where to place them in your home.

Crystal	Properties	Best Direction to Place It
Amethyst	Aids sleep; purifying and healing; encourages spiritual wisdom	Southwest, Northeast, or South
Citrine	Promotes optimism and a sunny outlook; good for a boost of happiness; dispels negative emotions	West, Northeast, Southwest, or Northwest
Emerald	Enhances psychic abilities; increases prosperity and financial abundance; improves communication skills and confidence	East or Southeast

Crystal	Properties	Best Direction to Place It
Jade	Attracts prosperity and good luck; protects against illness; promotes harmony	East or Southeast
Lapis lazuli	Has calming properties; protects against psychic attacks; increases clarity and objectivity	North
Opal	Promotes positivity; enhances creativity and aids in inspiration; has healing properties	Northwest
Rose quartz	Promotes harmony; enhances feelings of self-love and self-worth; improves emotional connections	Southwest, Northeast, or Center
Tiger's eye	Enhances clarity; reduces anxiety and self-doubt; motivational boost	West
White quartz	Has powerful healing properties; amplifies energy; aids concentration	West or Northwest

With so many crystals to pick from, how's a person supposed to choose?! Well, think carefully about what it is you may be struggling with at the moment. Do you feel in need of an energy boost, or maybe something to help ward off negative thoughts? Also remind yourself of the goals you wrote about in Chapter 3 and look through the chart to see which crystals best reflect what it is you're seeking to attract.

Once you have an idea of what kind of crystal would be best for you, visit your local crystal or rock shop. While shopping for crystals online certainly is more convenient for some, it's always best to be able to touch and hold crystals before you buy them. In addition, you'll be face to face with a shop assistant, who'll hopefully be able to answer any questions you may have.

Basic Crystal Care

As part of maintaining your crystals, they'll need to be cleansed regularly. Not only for practical reasons, such as to remove any dust or dirt that they may have gathered, but also to recharge the crystals' energy. In Feng Shui, crystals work hard to either absorb negativity or to attract positive energy, so regular cleansing helps "recharge their battery" and means that you're able to feel their benefits for the long term!

The first step is to cleanse them with water in any of the following ways:

♦ Give them a thorough rinse under the tap and clean them with lavender soap.

♦ Soak them in a bowl of saltwater to purify them (for about 20 minutes).

♦ Leave them outside the next time it rains—just remember to bring them back inside again!

You can make these methods more effective by visualizing the water cleansing away any negative energy. Remember to make sure your crystals are fully submerged in the water and to pat them gently dry afterwards.

The second step is to activate them:

♦ Place them outside in direct sunlight at noon on a bright, cloudless day to recharge under the sun's rays. Leave them out there for three hours, bringing them in at 3 p.m.

♦ When you bring them back in, activate the crystal with your intentions. With your eyes closed and your mind at rest, pick up your crystal and visualize a bright white light surrounding it. Think carefully about what it is you want your crystal to help you with and what it is you're looking to attract.

As for how often you should do this, it's recommended that you cleanse and reactivate your crystals:

♦ immediately after you first buy them to remove any energies of the previous owner

♦ at least once every six months after that

♦ any time you find yourself going through intense or emotionally difficult times, or when you feel as though your crystal has lost its radiance

In conclusion, crystals are very powerful and effective items to have in your Feng Shui toolbox. They don't necessarily require a heavy investment either, so feel free to experiment with some different types and see what works best for you.

CHAPTER 15

Activate Your Feng Shui with Plants and Flowers

Plants and flowers have long been used in Feng Shui as a quick and easy way to boost the energy of a room. Because they represent the wood element, they help promote positive health, growth, and boost the life force in the home.

What Are the Feng Shui Benefits of Houseplants?

What can be said about the amazing benefits of houseplants that hasn't been said before? Not only do they add a fresh splash of color to a room, but science has shown that they can help to increase oxygen levels, reduce tiredness, relieve stress, and can even boost your creativity.

In addition to these many health benefits, houseplants come with their own life force, which does wonders in keeping the flow of energy fresh and vibrant. Also, by bringing elements of the outdoor world into the inside, you're creating a more harmonious and balanced environment.

Which Houseplant Is Right for Me?

In general, it's best to go with lush, healthy plants with big, round leaves. Plants with spiky leaves and needles (such as succulents and cacti) are best avoided since the spikes disrupt and can "stab at" the flow of energy in a room. Going one step further, it's best to avoid even displaying any pictures or artwork of cacti. Think about it—where do you tend to find cacti? In the desert, which in turn can represent drought, famine, and fighting against nature to survive. Not exactly the sort of vibes you want to invite into your home!

As a guide, here is a list of some of the most popular houseplants and their properties:

Orchid
♦   considered to be a symbol of femininity and fertility

♦ represents purity and beauty

♦ can help improve romantic and family relationships

Money Tree

♦ used to attract wealth and abundance

♦ brings positive energy and good luck

Bamboo

♦ used to attract wealth and abundance

♦ considered to be very lucky

♦ symbolizes prosperity due to it being able to grow all year round

Jade Plant

♦ has soft, rounded leaves that attract good fortune

♦ symbolizes growth and renewal

♦ used to attract wealth and abundance

In order to get the positive energy benefits of houseplants, make sure that you're watering them enough and giving them the proper amount of sun exposure. If you find your plant looking like it's starting to die and no amount of sunlight or watering can revive it, it's best to dispose of it. Keeping a dead or dying plant can cause the energy of the room to become stale and lifeless.

What Are the Feng Shui Benefits of Flowers?

Who doesn't love to be greeted with a big bouquet of fresh flowers? Just like houseplants, their brightly colored petals and sweet scents can bring fresh new energy into a room.

Unlike houseplants, they have a much shorter life span. While a plant, if well looked after, can survive for a long time, even the most expensive bouquet of roses will naturally start to die after a relatively short time. There is something quite beautiful about this, though, as it serves as a reminder for us to cherish what we have in the here and now, and to enjoy the bloom of the flowers while we can.

What Flowers Are Best for Me?

Throughout history, flowers have been used to represent different things. Why does giving someone a dozen red roses send a totally different message to giving them a bouquet of daisies? Because we're taught that roses, particularly red ones, represent love, passion, and romance. Daisies, on the other hand, have more of a connection with childhood and innocence. This symbolism or "secret language" of flowers has been used in paintings, in poetry, and can even be seen in how we celebrate different holidays throughout the year. For example, we display daffodils during the springtime because they represent new beginnings and rebirth, and we decorate with poinsettias for Christmas since their cheery red leaves represent joy and festive cheer.

It's no different for Feng Shui. Depending on their color and petal-shape, different flowers can help to attract different things, such as a new romance or good fortune. Here is a list of the most popular flowers used in Feng Shui and their properties:

♦ Daffodils symbolize new beginnings, optimism, and good fortune.

♦ Hydrangeas symbolize gratitude.

♦ Lilies symbolize peace, calm, and well-being.

♦ Lotuses symbolize peace, harmony, and enlightenment.

- Peonies symbolize a new love. They can be used to help attract a new romance but it's important that once you're in a relationship, you dispose of the peonies; otherwise you may attract an additional, unwanted person into the relationship.

- Roses symbolize love, passion, and romance.

- Sunflowers symbolize positivity, joy, and lasting happiness.

- Tulips symbolize true love.

In Feng Shui, it is possible to use silk flowers instead of real ones and still get the same benefits. If you do choose to use real flowers, however, make sure to dispose of them when they start to die. Just as with houseplants, dead flowers can quickly turn the energy of a room from alive and vibrant to stale and stuffy. Similarly, dried flowers and potpourri are best avoided altogether since they can disrupt the positive flow of energy in the home.

CHAPTER 16

Activate Your Feng Shui with Water Features

Alongside fire, earth, air, and metal, water is one of the five elements in Feng Shui. While each element is important and should be represented in the home, water is especially important. The positive flow of energy moving throughout the home is very similar to a peaceful, slow-moving river, and so the presence of water helps to maintain this flow.

What Are the Feng Shui Benefits of Water?

Water is most strongly associated with abundance, meaning that having the right water feature in the right place in your home can help increase your wealth and cash flow. It can also bring about new opportunities and new directions in your career.

Activating with Water Inside the Home

The best way to represent the water element in your home is with a small water fountain. Not only are they available in a range of stylish designs to suit any taste, but the sounds of trickling water make for the perfect soothing soundtrack! As a rule of thumb, your water fountain should be kept clean and, when it's in use, the water should be constantly flowing. Make sure to adjust the speed so that the movement is calm and gentle—you want to avoid the sound of loudly splashing water.

Depending on where you place it, a water fountain can be used to attract different outcomes; for example:

◆ Placing one in the North area of your workspace (either your office or family room) can help to bring about new beginnings and opportunities in your career.

◆ Placing one in the Southeast area of your workspace can help attract abundance.

It's very important to avoid placing a water fountain in the bedroom. The active nature of a water feature can cause you to feel restless and make it hard for you to switch off at night. Similarly, you should also avoid having one in the kitchen since it can lead to you losing money.

Other Ways to Activate with Water

You can use aquariums to add the water element to a room. If a fish tank is placed in the North or Southeast area of the family room, for example, everyone in the home will be able to benefit from its money-attracting properties.

As for the fish you should place in there, if it's a small aquarium, try two gold-colored fish and one black-colored fish. If it's a larger aquarium, have eight gold-colored fish and one black-colored fish. The gold-colored fishes are there to attract abundance and the black-colored fish is there to absorb any negative energy. If you do decide to bring fish into your home, remember to respect them as the living, sentient creatures they are.

> It can be the case sometimes that the black-colored fish dies and keeps needing to be replaced. If this happens more than twice, it could be that you have some emotional issues about money that you need to work through. Do you have any hang-ups about money, any fears or negative thoughts about it? Do you have any unhealthy habits regarding money that you've picked up from your parents or those around you that you need to re-examine?

If it's not practical for you to add a water feature or aquarium to a room, displaying a photo or artwork of water can be an easy, no-fuss alternative. Here are some rules to keep in mind when selecting an image to display:

♦ Avoid images of waterfalls since the strength of the water represented in them can cause you to lose money very quickly.

♦ Avoid images of stormy seascapes with clouds or giant waves.

♦ Avoid images of still water or of boats anchored in a harbor. There needs to be a sense of movement in the water, otherwise money won't flow to you.

♦ Ideally, the image should depict a gentle moving river or ocean, perhaps with sailboats gliding on top.

Activating with Water Outside the Home

If you're lucky enough to have space for a large water feature, pond, pool, or hot tub in your backyard, these can also be used to attract abundance. The best location for anything involving water is in the East or the North, and ideally they should be at least 15ft (about 5m) from the house. Having "outside" water elements any closer to the home can have the effect of bringing about strong emotions in the people who live there.

CHAPTER 17

Feng Shui for Your Front Door

Now that you're familiar with the Feng Shui basics, let's begin to go through your home, room by room. We'll start this journey at the outermost part of your house: the front door and entrance area.

The entrance area is a powerful place, as it sets the tone for your whole home. It's where you first greet family and friends when you welcome them in, and it's the first space you pass through when you return home after a long day. It's also where energy enters your home, so you want this space to be as bright and welcoming as possible.

Take a moment to think about how you would like visitors to feel when they enter your home. Do you want your home to feel warm and inviting, or stylish, inspiring, and filled with beautiful things to look at? With this vision in mind, let's go over the Feng Shui dos and don'ts for this area.

Your Front Yard and Outside Area

This area may differ from home to home as some people may have large front yards complete with grass, plants, and trees, while other people may just have a concrete path leading up from the street to their front door.

If you're lucky enough to have a front yard, make sure that you're regularly mowing the grass, watering any flowers, and getting rid of any weeds. You want to keep everything looking neat and tidy. If you have a concrete pathway leading up to your door, make sure this is swept regularly.

It's important that this area is free from obstacles, so get rid of anything that people might trip over. Consider getting an outdoor light or a solar-powered lantern to keep the space well lit, even during the dark winter months.

Keep on top of any repairs that your front yard might need, including broken gates or mailboxes. For any trash cans that you keep outside, consider getting a covered storage area so that they're hidden from sight.

Your Front Door

As previously stated, you want to make sure there is a clear, obstacle-free path from the outside area leading up to your front door. This is because we want it to be as easy as possible for people (and positive energy!) to make it to the door. For this same reason, make sure that your house number is clearly displayed so that your door is easy to spot from the street. Also make sure that your doorbell is in working order because, after all, how can good fortune reach you if you can't hear it calling?

Clean your front door regularly with soap and water and keep it free from any chipped paint or scuffs.

A key Feng Shui must-have for your front door is a welcome mat, because not only does it send a very clear message of "you are welcome here," it enables your guests to wipe their shoes so they're not bringing dirt into your home. When picking out a welcome mat, go with anything that displays a warm, welcoming message and avoid mats that feature negative imagery (such as skulls) or novelty mats with messages like "go away" or "welcome to the madhouse." These may seem funny, but is that the kind of message you want to be sending to the Universe? Shake out the mat regularly and replace it at least once a year or when it starts to get holes in it.

If you regularly enter your home through a side or back door, give it the royal treatment by planting lush plants or flowers nearby. This way, you'll still feel as though you're a king or queen entering your "castle."

Your Entrance Area

This is the inside area that, when you open the front door, you directly step into. Usually, this space is used for storage and contains furniture such as coat racks, shoe racks, and side tables. Where possible, try to have enclosed storage (like a closet or cupboard with a door) so that you can hide your shoes and coats away. When you leave these things out in the open, this can symbolize a willingness to leave the home as quickly as possible, which is not something you want your guests to feel!

Make sure that there's nothing behind your front door to prevent you from being able to open it fully. Where possible, you want to make sure it opens to at least a 90-degree angle. Similarly, try to avoid obstacles like big side tables or storage boxes that you have to side-step as you walk through. To ensure a positive, easy flow of energy, you want the path through your home to be as clear as possible.

In this space, it's also important to keep personal objects to a minimum. The entrance area should be a neutral space in the home. You can place family photos to welcome guests into your family with open arms. Display photos or artworks that have positive imagery with light, bright colors. These can include beautiful painted landscapes or cheerful nature photography.

To keep the energy in this area fresh, never place a wastebasket or bin in your entrance area. Garbage cans pollute the new energy entering your home, so save them for the kitchen and bathroom.

If your entrance area doesn't have a lot of natural light, floor or table lamps can be used to illuminate the space instead. Place bunches of fresh flowers or green, leafy plants on any side tables, but make sure you throw them away (or better yet, compost them) when they start to die. If your entrance area feels cramped or narrow, hang up mirrors to create the illusion of more space. However, make sure that the mirror isn't facing the front door, since doing so could reflect all the incoming energy back outside your house!

When decorating this area, avoid painting it stark white and instead use light, warm tones. The bigger the space is, the deeper the color can be. Try to avoid deep greens, blues, reds, or purples, though.

Make sure that you dust any furniture in this area regularly, at least once a week. This includes cleaning any nearby mirrors or clocks. Dust any light fixtures or windows around the door so that the light is able to shine through as much as possible.

> **Clean your windows as they are the veil between you and the Universe. Dirty windows make it harder for you to see the beauty around you.**

If there are any nearby windows that you can open, do so regularly so that you're letting in the fresh air. If you're not able to open the windows, you can use air fresheners charged with essential oils. Again, you want to do whatever you can to make the best experience for anyone coming into your house.

CHAPTER 18

Feng Shui for Your Family Space

Next up is the family space, also known as the family room or living room. This is the area in the house where members of the household gather together to sit, relax, and enjoy each other's company. Since this is a shared space, our Feng Shui focus will be on promoting joy, harmony, and good communication between all who live in the home.

Family Room Furniture

The key piece of furniture that we will focus on in this room is the sofa. Unique to the family room, there are a few Feng Shui "must-dos" in regard to this item of furniture.

Firstly, it's important that there's enough room on the sofa for each person in the household to have a seat. If there's not, you can set out comfortable chairs nearby to add additional seating. By making sure that there's a seat for everyone, you'll be creating a welcoming and inviting space for all those who enter.

Secondly, it's important to have the sofa arranged so that those sitting on it don't have their back to the door that leads into this room. When sitting on the sofa, you should always have sight of the door, even if it's in your peripheral vision. Avoid placing the sofa in the middle of the room and instead have it positioned against a solid wall.

If you have additional chairs set out, you'll want to arrange those so that everyone is still facing each other when they sit down, and no one's sitting with their back turned to the other people in the room. Having everyone sit facing each other will help keep the conversation flowing and boosts that welcoming energy. After all, there's nothing more off-putting in a conversation than when you're talking to the back of someone's head!

As you can see in Figure 4, the sofa is positioned toward the center of the room so those sitting on it would have their backs to the door. They would also have their backs

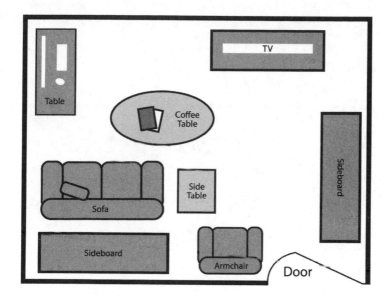

Figure 4: Bad family room layout

to whoever is sitting in the armchair behind them. Instead of a welcoming sofa and somewhere to sit, the TV is the first thing you see when you enter through the door and the room itself is filled with tables and cabinets that prevent a clear path for incoming energy to follow.

In Figure 5, the sofa is up against a wall and facing the door. The armchair placed next to it is also facing the door but it's angled in such a way that whoever is sitting on it is still part of the conversation with those sitting on the sofa. The TV isn't the focal point of the room and there is enough space for incoming energy to enter. The furniture doesn't clutter up the room, meaning the energy is free to flow.

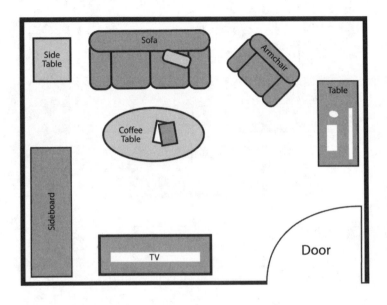

Figure 5: Good family room layout

In most homes, each member of the household will have their own designated space on the sofa or nearby where they always sit. It's important that the parents or the main breadwinner(s) are able to sit in the power position, with the clearest view of the door. This way, they'll be sitting in a welcoming stance to all those who walk through the door.

Lastly, if you're picking out a new sofa, it's important to think about which colors work best in Feng Shui:

♦ Earth tones such as beiges and browns are most successful.

♦ Green, yellow, orange, copper, and gray are also good choices.

♦ Avoid red, since its association with fire can lead to fiery tempers and heated arguments.

♦ I often find that people with blue sofas don't tend to sit on them much. The water energy that blues brings creates unstable energy, like sitting on water.

As for the other furniture in the room (such as coffee tables, side tables, and cabinets), try to avoid anything with sharp corners. Rounded corners or oval-shaped tables are best as they have no sharp corners to "stab" at the positive energy.

It's also important that the furniture is arranged so that the flow of energy isn't blocked. You want to be able to walk from one end of the room to the other without having to twist yourself around any obstacles in your way. There should be a clear, furniture-free path through the family room so that the incoming flow of energy has space to move.

As we've already learned, clutter is something to avoid at all costs in Feng Shui! Do make sure that your family room has adequate storage for things like books, DVDs, and toys so that these don't just pile up on the floor. Cabinets with doors and drawers are great since they keep everything out of sight, while a set of shelves or a bookcase will still be effective.

TV and Electronics

When you enter the room, the first thing you should see is the sofa, inviting you to sit down and relax. It's very important that your TV isn't the main focus of the room, so avoid placing it directly opposite the door.

Likewise, you don't want your TV surrounded by unsightly cables, wires, and other electrical equipment. The best solution is to have your TV sitting in a media unit, one that has doors or drawers to hide away unsightly cables, satellite boxes, and gaming consoles. Otherwise, you can always use cable ties to group the cables together and try to hide them out of sight.

Soft Furnishings

Peach and orange are both fabulous colors to use when it comes to attracting feelings of joy, harmony, and happiness. You can do this with peach or orange cushions, colored candles, or colored lamps. Salt lamps are also a great thing to have, with their soft orange lighting.

Avoid having too much red in the room, since all that fiery energy can cause tensions to run high. However, if you feel that people in the house are getting too lazy or need to pull their weight more, you can add red cushions to the sofa to add a little "get-up-and-go" boost to the energy flow!

You should also avoid having too much black and white in the room. Since these colors are at complete opposite ends of the color spectrum, they can prompt extreme high and low emotions and drastic mood swings.

> **Emerald green is the color of nature, a place where everything is growing and regenerating all the time. Place this color in the East area of your living room to help ensure your family stays healthy in body, mind, and spirit.**

Photos

In the family room, display separate photos of each member of the household in their respective Success Directions. In addition:

♦ Display photos of children with their mother or grandmother in the Southwest.

♦ Display photos of children with their father or grandfather in the Northwest.

♦ Display photos of your children or grandchildren in the West.

♦ Display photos of your ancestors or elder relatives in the East.

♦ Display photos of you with your romantic partner in your Relationship Direction.

Try to use as many recent photos as you can. Putting up old photos of yourself with your family or loved ones can cause your relationships to become "frozen in time" and stop them from moving forward. (This doesn't apply to wedding photos, though, since they celebrate a very important and sacred time in a couple's relationship.)

If you're hanging up other artworks in the room, make sure that these feature uplifting, joyful imagery. Before you display anything, just think: "Does this represent the sort of energy I want this room to have?" If it's a no, save it for another room, or maybe even consider donating it. As a general Feng Shui rule, avoid any images of weaponry, violence, war, or death. If you want to display any religious images or statues, place them in the Northeast.

Lighting

In regard to lighting, it's a very careful balancing act between having too much light and too little. You want to use as much natural lighting as possible, so leave the curtains open during the day and keep the windows clean and smudge-free. If you have heavy drapes that block out a lot of light, consider swapping them for ones made of a lighter fabric.

If you can, install dimmer switches for your overhead lighting so that you can adjust it for the perfect amount of brightness. Dark corners and shadowy rooms aren't good for Feng Shui, so arrange floor and table lamps so that when they're switched on, the whole room is softly illuminated. For best results, try placing one in each corner of the room.

Candles

Scented candles are a great way to boost the positive energy of the room. Vanilla candles or ones that smell like cookies are particularly good to have in the family room, since they help create a warm, cozy vibe. The smell of cookies in particular is very nostalgic—many of us have fond childhood memories that involve the smell of cookies in the oven! Burn the candle anytime you want to promote a sense of togetherness with those you live with.

Houseplants

Adding plants to a room is always a quick and easy way to bring in fresh, new energy. Not only do plants work to purify the air in a room, but they work to purify the energy. Choose plants with lush, round leaves and avoid spiky or pointy-leaved plants. These points disrupt the flow of energy, which can lead to conflict within the household. Orchids, with their beautiful blooms and soft leaves, are an ideal plant choice for the family room.

Crystals

Crystals can be used to promote a peaceful, loving energy in the room:

♦ White quartz can be used to calm the energy and maintain harmonious relationships in the home. It's also a good crystal to have nearby when you want to discuss difficult things with those you live with, such as boundaries, privacy, or chore division, and avoid any arguments.

♦ Rose quartz, particularly in the shape of a heart, is great for when you want to have gentle, encouraging conversations with your loved ones.

♦ Amethyst is used to promote transparency and communication. It's also beneficial for aiding forgiveness.

> **White is the color of purity and integrity. Anytime you feel like you need to let go of negative thoughts or feelings, place a white quartz crystal in the West of your living room to help you make decisions based on integrity.**

The Five Elements

Lastly, ensure that all five elements are represented in the room in order to create the most harmonious environment possible.

♦ Wood is represented by plants and flowers. Display these in either the East or Southeast, and also in the South.

♦ Water is represented by a water fountain or an aquarium. Display this in the North and also in the Southeast.

♦ Earth is represented by crystals. Display them in the Southwest, Northeast, or the Center of your home, and also in either the West or Northwest.

♦ Metal is represented by metal objects, such as a metal photo frame or a metal lamp. They can be displayed in the West or Northwest and also in the North.

♦ Fire is represented by candles or fireplaces. They can be displayed in the South and in the Southwest, Northeast, or the Center of your home.

By making all these small adjustments, you'll be able to create a home that is warm, nurturing, and perfectly in harmony.

CHAPTER 19

Feng Shui for the Master Bedroom

The three most important uses of the master bedroom are for rest, relaxation, and romance. Consider the bedroom your special space not only for sleeping and unwinding after a long day, but also for expressing your love for your partner. It should be peaceful, sensual, and free from anything that might disrupt a good night's sleep!

Your Bed

With respect to your bed, the two most important things to do are 1) to ensure that it's in the power position and 2) to ensure that, when you're sleeping, your head is facing one of your Personal Directions. Turn back to Chapter 5 for a recap on the power position and Chapter 6 for information on Personal Directions. There's also information in Chapter 6 on what to do if you and your partner have different Personal Directions.

As mentioned, make sure that your bed has a solid headboard and avoid one with slats. When you sit up, you want to be supported by the headboard itself and not be resting against the wall behind it. Not only is this far more comfortable for you, but in Feng Shui a solid headboard is also more effective for attracting money and abundance.

On top of your bed, make sure you have an even number of pillows, since an odd number can invite a third, unwanted person into the relationship. Decorative pillows are a great way to add a splash of color, as too much white can cause your emotional state to come to a standstill. If you're looking to boost your romance, choose pillows in pink or red, and if you're looking to improve your health, choose pillows in green or floral designs. Having stuffed toys on your bed is fine, too, but try to avoid any aggressive animals (like crocodiles, tigers, or sharks) and instead pick animals that mate for life or represent famous cartoon couples, such as Mickey and Minnie Mouse.

It has been said that storing things under the bed is a Feng Shui no-no, but I would disagree. So long as you're not storing anything under the area from your heart to your head when you're lying down and you can't actually see the boxes under the bed (you can always use a dust ruffle or bed skirt to keep them well-hidden), I would say that it's fine to make use of whatever storage space you can. Keeping clutter out of sight and to a minimum is definitely the priority!

If your bedroom has wooden beams on the ceiling, especially if they're above your bed, this can wreak havoc with your sleep. Remember that beams like this are what is known in Feng Shui as "poison arrows," meaning that they create fast-moving energy toward a person, cutting into their positive chi. You might find that you have trouble sleeping, or that you seem to wake up each day with pain in the part of your body that the beam is above. To help stop the negative effects of this poison arrow, paint the beam or cover it in the same colors as the ceiling so that it blends in.

66 *I had a client once who was an athlete. This young man was prone to suffering from leg injuries and he found them very hard to*

recover from. Looking around his bedroom, I saw that he was sleeping under a beam that ran horizontally above his legs! I told him to cover it with fabric as soon as possible and when I checked in with him again a few months later, he proudly announced that he hadn't had a leg injury since.

"

If you have an en-suite bathroom, make sure that you don't place your bed up against the wall of the bathroom, since then the energy of the bathroom would be too close to you while you sleep. Try to have your bed as far away from the bathroom wall as you can, or, if this isn't possible, place a mirror behind your headboard so that it's facing the bathroom in order to deflect the energy back.

Your Nightstand

As part of transforming your bedroom into a temple for love and romance, keeping things symmetrical is very important. Having two nightstands, one at either side of the bed, sends a message to the Universe that you respect the needs of your partner (this can be your current partner or a future partner). Similarly, make sure that there's a lamp on both nightstands and that both lamps are roughly the same size. If one person has a lamp that is much bigger or much brighter than the other, it can create a power struggle or a sense of inequality in the relationship.

Along with your lamp, you can set out an inspirational book or your journal, a scented candle with a romantic smell such as rose or jasmine, your favorite crystal, or framed photos of you with your loved one. Save any photos of you with your parents or children for another room—you don't want them to be watching over you while you're enjoying quality time alone with your partner! You should also avoid placing anything work-related on top of your nightstand, any dirty laundry, any models of cars, or any sort of weapon. It might be the case that you sleep with, for example, pepper spray or a baseball bat nearby for protection, but these objects attract a lot of fear-based energy, which can disrupt your peaceful sleep. Try to keep them as far away from where you sleep as is practically possible.

Although electric alarm clocks or cellphones are useful for those who need a little push to wake up in the morning, their electrical nature creates too much "fire" energy, which can in turn cause sleep problems. To avoid this, try to place your phone alarm clock at least 5ft (1.5m) away from the bed. This might seem strange, but it can actually be a useful life hack: If you have to physically get up and out of your bed to switch your clock or phone off, you're less likely to set it on snooze, roll over, and fall straight back asleep!

Your Storage

Make sure you have plenty of closet storage in your bedroom so you're not left with piles of laundry on the floor—everything should be hung up and put away. Ideally, your laundry basket should be placed in your bathroom, but if you're not able to do that, you should at the very least avoid putting it in any of your Personal Directions.

Likewise, keep exercise equipment, anything from treadmills to dumbbells, hidden away in a closet or cupboard when they're not in use, or cover them with a colorful sheet. The sight of an exercise bike is not exactly the thing to inspire a night's worth of rest and relaxation!

Your Desk

If you have a work desk in your bedroom, use a fold-out screen to hide it away while you sleep. Any work-related equipment, such as laptops, books, or briefcases should be stored away out of sight, too. Don't use a clear plastic box; instead, use a beautiful colored or patterned box so that it becomes a part of the decoration instead of the clutter. You want to give your brain the chance to switch off for the night, not to be surrounded by reminders of outstanding projects or tomorrow's to-do list.

Your Soft Furnishings

It's best to avoid having too many fire or water colors, such as reds and blues, in the bedroom, since they can make the energy of the room too active. Instead, metal colors (such as whites, golds, and silvers) and earth colors (such as beiges and browns) are better since they have a more calming effect on both mind and body. You can always stick to these color palettes for things like curtains, carpets, and bedsheets and then add pops of color with decorative pillows and other accessories.

To create a more sensual space, you can add fluffy rugs to either side of the bed so that when you and your partner first get out of bed, your feet are immediately greeted with softness. It's a great way to show yourself a little tenderness before you start your day!

If you're in a relationship, another important thing to keep in mind when deciding upon a color scheme or decorative style for the room is that both partners should be happy with the choices. For the energy to remain harmonious, both partners need to feel like they're equally represented. Be prepared to come to a few compromises and experiment with styles until you find something you both like.

Your Photos

One of the most important areas for displaying images in the bedroom is above the bed. Whatever image you place here can affect your dreams and quality of sleep. Here is a quick list of the types of images to avoid:

♦ Avoid anything with water, since having it above your head can create depressing thoughts.

♦ Avoid anything displaying single people or an odd number of people, since this can create disharmony in your relationship.

♦ Avoid anything displaying animals, particularly predators or violent animals, since this can attract stress, fear, and other negative emotions.

You should also avoid having shelves above your bed, since they can create a poison-arrow effect. Having a shelf filled with books is especially bad, because all those different stories can make it difficult for your mind to quieten down.

Instead, display a framed photo of yourself and your partner, a positive quote, or colorful illustrations of two hearts. I've seen people string twinkle lights around their bed, which I think is a beautiful way to transform a bed into a romantic space!

> **66** *I once had a famous acting couple come to me for some Feng Shui advice. While they got on very well for most of the day, they found that as soon as they got into bed, they would start fighting and arguing. It was beginning to affect their relationship, so I took a look around their bedroom. Above their bed, they had an image of two tigers. Granted, having two tigers is better than having one, but tigers are renowned for being quite aggressive lovers! They can't lie down together for long before they start fighting or trying to assert their dominance. I told them that if they changed the artwork for something a little more relaxing, their night-time arguments would soon be put to rest.* **99**

Mirrors

Mirrors are very powerful tools in Feng Shui and, as we've seen in previous chapters, can be a welcome addition to many rooms in the home. The bedroom, however, isn't one of them!

When you have a mirror or reflective surface (including the shiny, black screen of a TV or computer on standby) opposite or at the side of your bed, you're also "doubling" your body, which can double any current health issues you may have (including physical, emotional, and mental problems). Not only that, but it can lead to bad dreams, problems sleeping, and it can even have a negative effect on your relationship. If you're sharing a bed with a partner, a mirror across from the bed can lead to unwelcome people becoming involved in the relationship, whereas if you're single, it can double the sense of loneliness that you feel.

A quick and easy fix for this is to cover any mirror or shiny surface with a scarf, curtain, or a fold-out screen while you sleep. You can also paint over the mirrored surface if you're able to, or you can even just move it away so that it's not positioned directly across from the bed!

Plants

Similarly, while plants are an excellent way to add fresh, new life force into a room, this can be too much for the bedroom. The high amount of energy that plants bring can be too intense in a room meant for sleep and relaxation. They can trick your body into thinking that it's out in nature and that it needs to stay alert, so save the greenery for another room. You can always stick to fake plants or silk flowers if you want to add a touch of color!

Other Accessories

Water elements such as a water fountain or aquarium are also a no-no in the bedroom, since they can create too much energy. The flowing water creates too much motion, too much movement, and can lead to nights spent tossing and turning. Not to mention that the sound of all that water can have you waking up regularly for trips to the bathroom!

If you want to create a relaxing mood, have scented candles or air fresheners set out around the room. Launder your bed sheets regularly so that they're kept crisp and clean, and get into the habit of giving the room a quick five-minute tidy before you get ready for bed. A peaceful bedroom equals a peaceful night's sleep.

If you have pets, it's not good Feng Shui-wise to keep them in the bedroom, especially if they're in a cage (like a hamster or a dog in a crate) or in a tank (like fish or a lizard). It's pretty bad symbolism and can leave you feeling "trapped" in your relationship. Avoid it if possible, or, if you can't, avoid placing the cage or tank in one of your Personal Directions and keep it as far away from your bed as possible.

> **"** *I had a client once who loved to collect statues and figurines of angels. She had at least a hundred of them displayed all over her house and bedroom. She'd asked for my help because she hadn't had a partner in a very long time, and she was looking to attract a new romance into her life. Well, I told her that while angels did indeed represent love, it was more of a pure, innocent love. They loved, but they didn't make love, so having so many displayed in her bedroom was sending out the wrong message to the Universe about what she wanted. I told her to give away the majority of the angels to her friends, family, and those around her. She decided to give some of the angels to a group of people who sang at her local church and went on to marry one of the men in this group.* **"**

CHAPTER 20

Feng Shui for the Children's Bedroom

Whether you're the parent of a newborn baby or of a teenager in their last year of high school, there are some extra things you need to think about with the Feng Shui of your child's (or children's) bedroom(s). While the focus on the master bedroom is all about creating a space for rest and romance, the focus on a child's bedroom is all about helping them to find their own identity. It should be a space for creativity, playing, and learning about the world around them. Most importantly, though, you want it to be a space for them to feel safe in. Growing up can be scary at times, so it's important that your child views their room as somewhere they can go to feel safe, secure, and reminded of the love you have for them.

Because children can fall into a wide age range, some of the advice below will only apply to much younger children, while other pieces will only apply to older teenagers. As a general rule, if your child is above the age of 14, it's a good idea to ask their permission before you Feng Shui their bedroom. You can use this as a starting point to have a talk with your child about what their dreams and ambitions are, what their goals are, and what areas of their life they would like help improving. During this conversation, make sure you're really listening and focusing on what they're telling you, and be sure to respond from a place of love. You may find that this Feng Shui exercise brings you both closer together than before!

If you find that your child doesn't want you to Feng Shui their bedroom, be gentle. Ask them why and try to respond reasonably to any concerns they may have. A good deal could be that they allow you to Feng Shui their room and they keep it that way for nine days, at which point if they're still not happy, you promise to move everything back as it was. I strongly believe, however, that when they see how much their life has improved in just that short space of time, they'll be happy with the changes!

Their Personal Directions

Activating your child's Personal Directions is just as important as activating your own, but it's important that this is done in a more child-friendly way. Instead of focusing on attracting money or a new career by activating their Success Direction, you can activate it for success at school or with a sports team they're a member of. Instead of attracting romance, activate their Relationship Direction to improve their family relationships or attract a better friendship group at school. Again, if your child is old enough, take the time to talk with them to see what it is they would like to attract and work that into the activation of their Directions.

In their Success Direction, display their name and an up-to-date photo of them on a pin board. Pin up their paintings or artwork, display any awards, certificates, or ribbons they may have won, and arrange images that relate to their interests and career goals. For example, you could pin up photos of their favorite soccer player if they want to be a soccer player themselves, or book covers from their favorite genre if they want to become a writer.

In their Relationship Direction, display a framed photo of them with their parents, a framed photo of them with their siblings, and a framed photo of them with their school class or sports team. Be sure to update these photos regularly so that the relationships don't become "frozen" in time.

In their Health Direction, display anything relating to whichever sport or physical activity that they do. For example, if you have a photo of them performing at a ballet recital or at a baseball game, display that here in a colorful frame.

Finally, in their Wisdom Direction, place a bookcase and fill it with a range of age-appropriate books. Be sure to include both non-fiction and fiction so that your child can enjoy learning about the world around them and also boost their powers of imagination. If your family practices a religion, this is also a good area in which to display any holy texts, statues, or objects.

The Bed

A child's bed needs to be placed in a power position while also making sure that when they're sleeping, their head is facing one of their Personal Directions. However, unlike the bed in the master bedroom, a child's bed can be pushed right up against the side wall since they won't be looking to attract a partner. When your child is old enough to start dating and you both decide that it's the right time, you can move the bed out from the wall so that there's room for a nightstand on the other side.

As explained earlier, there should be no shelves above your child's bed. If you choose to have a photo or picture displayed above the bed, make sure it doesn't show anything too energetic or dangerous. Pictures of running people or animals, cars, or anything in motion can give off too much energy and make it hard for your child to go to sleep. Similarly, pictures of dangerous wild animals or anything with violent imagery can cause them to have nightmares. Best to stick to a peaceful nature scene or an inspiring photo of their idol.

Their Desk

If you have school-aged children who have homework to do each night, it's a good idea for them to have a work desk in their bedroom. Make sure it's positioned facing the door and use a fold-out screen to hide it away or cover it with a blanket when it's not in use. This helps to protect the balance of energy in the room—they might have trouble sleeping if they have their desk in full sight, piled high with their homework for the weekend!

Their Soft Furnishings

With a child's room, you can get away with using brighter colors than in an adult's room. If your child has more feminine energy, you can use pinks, whites, and golds; and if your child has more male energy, yellows and oranges work best. It's best to avoid having too much black in the room as this can cause depressive energy, especially amongst older children and teenagers, who are generally more likely to experience mood swings.

Particularly with younger children, murals or illustrated wallpaper are popular choices for decorating the room. This can be a great way to add a cheerful touch to the area, but just keep in mind what the illustrations represent. While they may seem cute, animals like tigers, lions, or dinosaurs are violent predators and therefore probably not the best things to be keeping watch over your child! Cars, particularly racing cars, are also a popular choice for wallpaper, murals, and even bed-sheet patterns. Again, they may seem cute but having bed sheets printed with a cartoon car is symbolic of placing your child *under an actual car*! Avoid having cars on bed sheets altogether and if you really must have illustrations of them on the walls, keep these as far away from the bed as possible.

Generally, less is more when it comes to posters or artwork in a child's room. No matter how much they like cars, horses, or their favorite pop singer, they don't need 30 posters hanging on the wall! In the same way that cupboards or closets can become cluttered, a wall with too much hanging artwork can become cluttered as well. Keep space in between the photos and pictures so the energy still has room to flow freely.

Their Toys

If your child is still at the age where they have toys, make sure they have special storage space to hide them away in. This can be a drawer, a closet, or a toy box (just so long as it's not see-through). Encourage them to get into the habit of putting everything away at the end of playtime, since having toys scattered around the room can make it harder for a child to calm down and relax, especially before bedtime. Additionally, scattered toys can cause the energy to become slow and sluggish, just like any other kind of clutter in the home. By teaching your child the importance of good organization and keeping things clutter-free, you're teaching them good, lifelong Feng Shui habits!

With this in mind, it's also good practice to encourage your child to sort through their toys regularly and donate anything they've outgrown or no longer play with. Annoyingly, toys are quite easy to break, so set aside time to either fix anything that's broken or to get rid of it entirely.

CHAPTER 21

Cooking and Dining with Good Feng Shui

In a lot of people's opinions, the kitchen is one of the most important rooms in the home. Think about it: If you've ever gone over to someone's house for a party, I bet you've ended up at some point in the kitchen! It's the unofficial heart of the home, and it's easy to see why. It's a place of warmth and comfort. It's where we go to make delicious meals to feed ourselves and others.

In terms of Feng Shui, the kitchen is closely related to money and your cash flow. A lot of the Feng Shui "must-dos" for the kitchen relate to creating a space that honors and respects food, because this in turn shows that you honor and respect your money. If you have a fridge full of moldy food, a stove caked in grease, and cabinets filled with broken pots and pans, don't be surprised if your money situation becomes equally messy.

Oven, Stove, and Microwave

In Feng Shui, both your oven and microwave are what are known as "mouths of chi," meaning a place that energy flows in from. To make the most of this incoming flow of fresh energy, it's best to have them facing the family breadwinner's Health Direction, or one of their other three Personal Directions. Since most ovens are built-in and tricky to move, you can always reposition the microwave to face this direction as an easy alternative instead.

It's also good to have the stove positioned so that when a person is standing in front of it, they're facing one of the four Personal Directions of either the family breadwinner or the person responsible for the majority of the cooking.

A key thing to remember is to keep all these appliances clean and to wipe down the counters each time they've been used. Remember, dirt and grime can cause the energy to become stale and, in a room so closely linked to money, it's important to keep the energy fresh and flowing.

Fridge

The best kind of fridge is one that's clean and organized, so make sure you're clearing it out properly at least once a week. If you have any leftovers sitting on the shelf for more than a week, accept that you're not going to eat them and throw them away! Wash the shelves with warm, soapy water to keep them clean and free from bits of old food. Organize your fridge so there's a section for fruits, for vegetables, for dairy products, and for meat and fish. There are a number of cheap plastic storage solutions on the market, such as trays and air-tight containers, especially designed to help with this.

It may be tempting to place photos of your family and friends on your fridge, but that's not a good idea according to Feng Shui. You don't want to risk the cold energy from the fridge "freezing" your relationships with them. Instead, display things that inspire you. I find that fridge magnets collected from your travels are an excellent thing to display—they're fun, colorful, and can inspire you to maintain your adventurous spirit.

> I knew someone who displayed a list of their goals on the fridge. Once I found out, I immediately told her to move it: Didn't she know that she was putting all her dreams and future goals "on ice"?!

Kitchen Cupboards and Pantry

When was the last time you went through all your cupboards and pantries? Expired food is not just a potential health hazard, it can also negatively impact the energy flow of your home in a major way.

Go through everything inside and remove anything that's expired, moldy, or just looks or smells a little off. Wipe clean the surfaces with some fresh-smelling cleaning products and then replace all the products that are still in date back onto the shelves. If you have any canned or dried goods that are still within their expiration date, but that you know you won't get around to using, consider donating them to a local food bank or shelter. Aim to clear out your pantry like this once every three months.

Kitchen Island

If you have a kitchen island, treat it in the same way as you'd treat a dining room table. Make it inviting with fresh flowers and candles, and ensure that you wipe it down after each time you eat.

Avoid displaying bowls of loose change, papers, or bills on the island. In fact, avoid bringing any money or money-related items into the kitchen. In Feng Shui, the sink represents money flowing out of the household, so it's best not to leave any money in this room of the house. You should also avoid paying any bills (either on the phone, by check, or online) in the kitchen, too.

Plates and Cutlery

Did you know that, according to Feng Shui, different color plates can have different effects on you?

♦ Beige, brown, or earth-toned plates are good for aiding interesting and lively conversation between diners.

♦ White plates, particularly with a silver or gold trim, promote celebration and success. Consider using white plates like this for your next business dinner or party.

♦ Blue and black plates can aid in weight loss and help encourage healthy eating.

In general, avoid using red plates. Red represents fire, so eating off this color earthenware can lead to health issues and inflammation.

Also, avoid using plastic or paper plates and cutlery when eating. Even if you're eating take-out, take the time to transfer the food from the take-out container over to a proper plate. Can you imagine a king or queen eating with a plastic fork, grabbing helpings from a cardboard pizza box? Of course not! Again, it's all about the little, mindful things you can do to show that you're respecting and honoring your food and, in turn, your money.

As for cutlery, stainless steel or silver-colored knives and forks are best. Silver helps to magnify energy, so this kind of cutlery is particularly good for special meals and dinner parties since it will help to amplify the good vibes.

Knives

It might seem like a strange thing to focus on, but the correct placement of your kitchen knives (the ones you use to chop and prepare food with, not the ones you eat with) is very important in Feng Shui. Remember how in Chapter 15, it was mentioned that cacti and plants with pointed leaves are best avoided? Knives, with their sharp points, "stab" at and disrupt the flow of positive energy in much the same way.

The best option is to keep your knives hidden in a cupboard or a drawer. If this isn't possible, you should at least have them positioned in such a way so that they're not visible when you walk through the door.

Towels

The best colors for your kitchen towels, oven mitts, and soft furnishings depend on the direction of your kitchen in the home. To find this out, simply stand in the center of your house with either the Diamond Compass on your phone or a physical compass in front of you at heart level, and then see which direction lines up with your kitchen door.

♦   For South-facing kitchens, use red.

♦   For Southwest- or Northeast-facing kitchens, use yellow or orange.

♦   For North-facing kitchens, use blue or black.

♦   For Southeast- or East-facing kitchens, use floral prints or stripes.

♦   For West- or Northwest-facing kitchens, use yellow, orange, gray, or beige.

♦   For kitchens that are in the center of the home, use yellow or orange.

Photos

Avoid displaying any family photos in the kitchen. Since the room deals with a lot of conflicting water and fire energy, this can lead to turbulent relationships and arguments within the family. Instead, display images of things that will help inspire you while cooking, such as artwork featuring fruits, vegetables, flowers, herbs, and other types of food.

Houseplants

Finally, similar to how growing fresh plants and herbs in your garden is an excellent way to boost the energy and keeps things smelling fresh there, having something growing in the kitchen, like herbs, can help your money to "grow," too. Add fresh homegrown herbs to your cooking whenever possible; they'll help you create dishes that are good for the taste buds and good for the soul!

Your Dining Area

Whether you have a dining room or a dining table in the kitchen, you want this area to be comfortable, inviting, and appealing to the senses.

Dining Table

As is the case in Feng Shui, curved and rounded edges are preferable over sharp, pointed ones. A symmetrical, round dining table, or a square or rectangular one with rounded corners is best. However, if you have a table with sharp and pointed edges, you can put a tablecloth over it to help soften the corners and prevent the energy from getting "caught" on them.

In terms of materials, wood, granite, and ceramic are best since they all represent the earth element. As food also represents earth energy, you're helping to avoid any conflicting energies. Glass-top tables aren't a good choice since they can represent things "falling through," and metal tables are another bad choice, since the metal can disrupt the energy of the food. If you do happen to have a glass or metal table, a tablecloth can be used to help neutralize the energy.

On top of the table, set out a bowl of fresh fruit, a bouquet of flowers, or a lush plant. This helps to attract abundant energy and bring some fresh life force into the room.

It's a good idea to set out placemats on the table whenever you serve a meal. Not only does this help on a practical level to avoid food stains on the tablecloth, but you can use different colored placemats to help attract different things. Gold or silver placemats are good at enhancing the celebratory energy at special dinners, and for more general everyday dining, beige, brown, yellow, or orange placemats are good for maintaining calm, restful energy. Red placemats often lead people to eat more food at a quicker rate, while blue placemats can help people to eat less.

When a meal is served, try to have the five elements represented on the table to help balance the energy in the room. You don't need to do this for every single meal, but it's a good idea to do so for special dinners, celebratory dinners, or dinners marking holidays and important dates.

♦ To represent water, set out some fresh water in a glass carafe.

♦ To represent metal, set out stainless steel cutlery.

♦ To represent earth, set out ceramic plates or serving bowls.

♦ To represent fire, set out a candle (any color will do).

♦ To represent wood, set out a vase of fresh flowers.

As part of creating a comfortable atmosphere, having a soft, fluffy carpet or rug under the dining table is a nice extra touch. If you've ever found your feet resting on a hard, cold floor, you know how uncomfortable it can be! A fluffy rug is a quick and simple thing you can do to add a touch of luxury to the dining area.

Dining Chairs

Make sure your dining chairs are high-backed and supportive. If you're able to have dining chairs with armrests, even better, but a solid back is an absolute must. You want those sitting around the table to feel comfortable enough to remain there for however long they want. Cushions or seating pads are a fairly inexpensive way of increasing the comfort of older dining chairs that may feel a little worn out.

When it comes to figuring out who sits where at the table, make sure that the head of the family (in most cases this will be the breadwinner) is sitting in the power position at the table. It's very important that any children at the table are not sitting in the power position, or at least not sitting in a power position if the breadwinner isn't, since this can be seen as a sign of disrespect. Children don't run the household and they certainly shouldn't be calling the shots, so consider switching up the household seating plan if you need to make things more balanced.

Photos

When you're eating in your dining area, you want to feel as though you're dining in a palace or an exclusive, high-end restaurant. This means that you want to create a space that looks and feels luxurious and indulgent, a real treat for the senses. It should be a feast for the eyes as much as it is a feast for the stomach!

The rules about what you can and can't display in the dining area aren't as strict as in the other areas of the house, but generally you want to avoid images of guns, war, conflict, or dead animals (this includes displaying horns or taxidermy). It's also best not to display photos of any relatives who have passed away. This space is about celebrating what it means to be alive—eating, drinking, and being merry with your loved ones around you. It's best to avoid dining amongst the dead.

So, with a little more creative freedom at your disposal, display your most beautiful pieces of artwork in gold or silver frames. Set out vibrant flowers in beautiful vases and invest in quality napkins and tablecloths that are soft to the touch. You want this space to say "luxury gourmet dining," not "local fast-food joint"!

CHAPTER 22

Feng Shui for Your Bathroom

Finally, we have the bathroom. An important but often ignored room of the house, it can be a space for self-reflection, self-care, or just somewhere you can grab five minutes of peace while you take a shower!

While it might be the place that people spend the least amount of time in, the bathroom still has an important purpose and deserves that "Feng Shui touch" just like the other rooms in the home.

Ideally, you want to avoid having a bathroom directly opposite the front door of your home. Since the front door is where all the fresh, new energy enters from, you don't want to direct that energy straight into the bathroom.

If you do happen to have a bathroom in this position, try placing a mirror on the front of the bathroom door to give the energy a chance to relocate.

It's also not ideal, Feng Shui-wise, to have an en-suite bathroom. This is because you don't want to have the relaxing, romantic energies of the bedroom mixing with the potentially unclean energies of the bathroom. To get around this, make sure that the en-suite door is kept shut at all times. Not only is this essential for privacy and for keeping the toilet out of sight, it helps ensure that you're not contaminating your home's positive energy with any stale energy from the bathroom.

Worse still is if you have any bathroom "elements" like a sink in your bedroom, as this again can cause the room's energy to become imbalanced. To help, keep these things hidden (especially while you sleep) with a curtain or a portable screen.

Bath, Toilet, Shower, and Sink

One of the most commonly asked questions I receive as a Feng Shui Master is, "Should I leave the toilet seat up or down?" Who knew that the humble toilet could be the source of such confusion!

Now, there are some forms of Feng Shui that say that leaving the toilet seat up flushes away all your positive energy, or "chi." Honestly, it doesn't actually make too much of a difference. Instead, your main focus should be on making sure your toilet is regularly scrubbed clean and that there is sweet-smelling air freshener nearby. Lavender is a particularly good essential oil for purifying energy, so look for an air freshener with that scent. Similarly, scented candles are great to keep in the bathroom. Aim for calming scents like vanilla, or something uplifting like mint or pine.

Speaking of smells, it's very important to have a good air-filtration system in the bathroom. This can be in the form of a fitted extractor fan, or just remembering to keep the window open during the day to let in the fresh air. Not only does this help get rid of any nasty, lingering odors, but it helps to keep the positive energy circulating. Additionally, green leafy plants can be added to purify the air in the room.

As for bathtubs and sinks, it's safe to say that they can become very dirty, very quickly. From plugholes blocked with hair to stained bathtubs, this dirt can cause the energy of the home to become stale, lifeless, and even cause conflict between those in the home. Purify any potential unclean energy by giving the toilet, sink, shower or bathtub, and the floor a good clean at least once a week.

Another key thing to keep in mind is how much water you are using. Not just for Feng Shui but also for the sake of the planet, it's important that we are mindful of only using as much water as we need. With an increasing number of towns and cities experiencing droughts and water shortages, play your part by making sure you're not wasting any unnecessary water. Check your pipes regularly for leaks, consider a water-saving device for your toilet cistern, or even just set a time limit on your showers. Acting for the good of the planet is an easy way to generate some positive energy for your home!

Bathroom Cabinet

Go through and eliminate any clutter from your bathroom cabinets or cupboards on a regular basis. Grab a trash bag and throw out anything that's expired or empty. If you have makeup, skincare, or hair products that you bought on a whim but never used again, see if you can give them to your friends or family instead.

For your remaining products, there are plenty of inexpensive storage options to pick from. You can try a cabinet, a freestanding set of drawers, or even just a pretty dish to set your products on. Just so long as there's a designated place for everything.

If you're looking to attract a new partner or romance in your life, you can use your bathroom storage as part of your manifestation. Set aside storage space in your cabinets and drawers for your future partner's toiletries too. Hang up towels just for them and set out a spare toothbrush for them to use. By making the effort and taking these extra steps, you're showing the Universe that you already have the space in your life for someone new.

Soft Furnishings

Blue, green, and white are excellent colors to have in your bathroom. Blue represents cleansing, green represents healing, and white represents purity, and those are all things you definitely want to have represented in your bathroom! Pick out towels, bath mats, blinds, or curtains in these colors.

Photos

Make sure not to display any photos of your family and loved ones, your trophies, or statues of any religious figures in this space. You must have heard stories about award-winning actors placing their Oscars in their bathroom, but this is really bad Feng Shui. Think about it: Is the bathroom really the place you want to display to the Universe all the things that you hold dear? Instead, display pretty photos of things like flowers and nature scenes.

Mirrors

Mirrors are a definite bathroom essential when you're flossing your teeth, applying makeup, or shaving your beard. Just make sure that any mirror you hang up or place on a counter is not reflecting the toilet in any way. As mentioned before, mirrors will double the energy of whatever they reflect, so you really don't want it to be pointed toward that!

CHAPTER 23

Feng Shui for Traveling and the Holidays

Now that we've gone over all the basics, this chapter will cover how to use Feng Shui for two different common scenarios: when you're away from home traveling and when you are celebrating the holidays at home.

Traveling

Whether it's an around-the-world cruise or a road trip across the country to visit distant relatives, there's nothing like travel to create precious, lifelong memories. To support you on your travels, there are plenty of Feng Shui tips and tricks to help ensure a safe journey, full of luck, opportunity, and adventure.

Before You Leave

Alongside packing your suitcase and double-checking your flight details, here are some Feng Shui "must-dos" that you should be including on your preparation checklist:

♦ Make sure that all the beds in the house have been made up with freshly washed sheets before you set out. A crumpled, dirty bed can disturb the energy in a room, so be sure to leave it looking tidy. Besides, think how good it will feel to fall asleep on crisp, clean sheets when you return home!

♦ Avoid leaving piles of clothes on the floor after you've finished packing. Place anything that you're not taking with you back neatly in your closets and drawers. As you should know by now, clutter is a big Feng Shui no-no, so spend a little extra time making sure everything is tidied away.

♦ Clear out your fridge to ensure that you're not leaving any perishable items in it while you're away. This includes things like fruit and vegetables, milk and dairy products, and anything that has a "use by" date that will expire while you're away. Freeze what you're able to and donate the rest to friends, family, or neighbors.

♦ Keep things smelling sweet while you're away by placing air fresheners in your bathroom and bedroom. Place scented candles around your home, too, and light them as soon as you return.

In Your Hotel Room

♦ Carry a pack of scented wipes if you ever need to freshen up your room. Lavender in particular is great for purifying a new area.

♦ When checking into your hotel room, ask if you can have a room away from busy elevators, stairwells, and outside traffic or construction. Not only will this lead to a quieter and more peaceful sleep, but having lots of people moving about near you can disrupt the energy of the room. Ask politely, and be sure to thank the hotel staff for their help.

♦ Furniture with sharp corners can interfere with the flow of energy, so drape scarves or bathroom towels around the sharp corners of any bedside tables or dressing tables in the room.

♦ If there's a mirror opposite the bed, cover it at night with a scarf or bathroom towel. Sleeping with a mirror across from you is bad Feng Shui and can cause a range of problems—from nightmares and insomnia to low energy. Not what you need during a week of sightseeing!

> If you're staying with friends or family on your travels, always be sure to bring a gift for your hosts. Something sweet and homemade, like freshly baked cookies or cakes, is perfect for showing how thankful you are for their hospitality.

When You Return

♦ The very first thing you want to do when you return is to open up the windows and let the fresh air in. This allows the energy to start flowing in your home again and gets rid of all the stale air that's been collecting while you've been away.

♦ Play some cheerful music to welcome some happy energy into your home after it has stood silent and empty for a while.

♦ When you've unpacked and settled back into your home, buy a bouquet of fresh flowers. Put them in a vase and display them in your living room, adding a splash of color and new energy to the room.

♦ Light a candle in your favorite scent to freshen the air and make your home smell like "you" again.

Staying Home for the Holidays

Celebrating the holidays at home can be such a fun, joyous thing, but let's face it—it can also be a source of stress! From hosting family members to putting together a feast that caters to both your vegan sister and your vegetable-hating younger cousins, having everything run smoothly can be a juggling act.

Luckily, Feng Shui offers the perfect solutions. From the colors of the napkins to the decorations you display, you can activate the energy in your home to guarantee a holiday season that's filled with love.

How to Decorate Your Place of Celebration

The color scheme and the type of decorations you should use depend on the direction of the room in which you'll be celebrating (for most people, this will be the living or family room, but it can also be the dining room).

If your place of celebration is in the South:

♦   Decorate with reds, purples, oranges, and hot pinks. You can use these colors for tablecloths, napkins, candles, or decorative accessories.

♦ Include triangle-shaped decorations and flashing twinkle lights.

♦ Use red, orange, hot pink, or purple wrapping paper and ribbons for any gifts you exchange with family or friends.

If your place of celebration is in the Southeast:

♦ Decorate with golds, blues, and purples. You can use these colors for tablecloths, napkins, candles, or decorative accessories.

♦ Include bells and tear-shaped ornaments, alongside anything that's shining and sparkling.

♦ Place a sprig of mistletoe on the ceiling.

♦ Use gold, green, blue, or purple wrapping paper and ribbons for any gifts you exchange with family or friends.

If your place of celebration is in the East:

♦ Decorate with light blues and silvers. You can use these colors for tablecloths, napkins, candles, or decorative accessories.

- Include bells and tear-shaped ornaments, alongside anything antique or sparkly.

- Place a sprig of mistletoe on the ceiling.

- Use light blue, green, or silver wrapping paper and ribbons for any gifts you exchange with family or friends.

If your place of celebration is in the West or Northwest:

- Decorate with golds, silvers, whites, oranges, and yellows. You can use these colors for tablecloths, napkins, candles, or decorative accessories.

- Include round, shiny, or star-shaped ornaments.

- String up star-shaped twinkle lights.

- Use white, gold, or silver wrapping paper and ribbons for any gifts you exchange with family or friends.

If your place of celebration is in the Southwest:

- Decorate with pinks, reds, oranges, and yellows. You can use these colors for tablecloths, napkins, candles, or decorative accessories.

♦ Include square or rectangular-shaped ornaments.

♦ String up colored twinkle lights or lights in the shape of candles.

♦ Hang up a gold and red garland.

♦ Use all sorts of pink and red wrapping paper and ribbons for any gifts you exchange with family or friends.

If your place of celebration is in the Northeast or in the Center of the home:

♦ Decorate with yellows, oranges, and warm reds. You can use these colors for tablecloths, napkins, candles, or decorative accessories.

♦ Include square or rectangular-shaped ornaments.

♦ String up colored twinkle lights or lights in the shape of candles.

♦ Hang up a gold or red garland.

♦ Use yellow, purple, orange, and red wrapping paper and ribbons for any gifts you exchange with family or friends.

If your place of celebration is in the North:

♦ Decorate with blues, whites, silvers, and golds. You can use these colors for tablecloths, napkins, candles, or decorative accessories.

♦ Use blue, white, silver, and gold wrapping paper and ribbons for any gifts you exchange with family or friends.

The holidays are the perfect time to celebrate all that you have to be grateful for in your life, so don't forgot to share some of your newfound luck and abundance. Check in with your local charities or shelters to offer donations or your services as a volunteer. Be kind to those around you and perhaps make it a challenge of yours to perform a random act of kindness each day in the run-up to the big day—just the thing to pass on a little festive cheer!

CONCLUSION

The rooms in your home are decluttered, your bed is facing in the power position, and you've activated all your Personal Directions… what now? It may seem like you've reached the end of your Feng Shui journey, but really, this is only the beginning.

From reading the pages of this book, you should now have a solid understanding of the basic principles of Feng Shui and how to apply them; what you have to do now is to build on that. There are many additional layers to Feng Shui and there are still so many exciting new things for you to discover.

EXERCISE

To help you reflect on all the things you've learned, here is a series of questions for you to answer. This is a safe place for your thoughts, so in a journal or a notebook write truthfully and in as much detail as you can:

◇ What are the key changes that you've made in your home?

◇ What do you still have left to do?

◇ How have you felt during this process? Were there times where you felt overwhelmed, unsure, or upset? What did you do to work through those feelings?

◇ What positive effects have you started to notice as a result of beginning your *Feng Shui Your Life* journey?

◇ In what ways have you already shared this information with your friends and family, and in what ways will you go about doing this in future?

◇ What are the top five habits you've picked up from this book that you will continue to do as part of your *Feng Shui Your Life* journey?

◇ Do you feel ready to take the next steps?

ADDITIONAL RESOURCES

To help you on your way, I've written a number of books on Feng Shui and the Law of Attraction principles associated with it. You can find them on Amazon, available in both printed and eBook format.

The Energy Number Book

We all know that every person is different, so why should there be a one-size-fits-all Feng Shui approach?

In *The Energy Number Book*, readers will learn a fresh, new approach in the form of the phenomenally effective Personal Energy Number system.

With each chapter devoted to a different Personal Energy Number and divided into success, health, relationships, and inner wisdom advice, this step-by-step guide is just the thing for those looking to add more "oomph!" to their Feng Shui. You'll learn tips and tricks, tailor-made to your Energy Number, which will help you to manifest the life of your dreams quickly and effortlessly.

The Diamond Energy Principles

If you've ever been curious about the Law of Attraction and how it could work for you, *The Diamond Energy Principles* will be a welcome new addition to your bookshelf!

This book covers each of the 24 Diamond Energy Principles and outlines how to use them to quickly and effortlessly manifest the future you desire.

Divided into four main sections—success, health, relationships, and inner wisdom—this book gives you the tools you need in order to make your dreams a reality. Each chapter comes with detailed and easy-to-understand explanations, Feng Shui tips, and effective visualization exercises.

The Diamond Energy Journal

Discover just how easy it is to transform your life with this unique journaling experience! *The Diamond Energy*

Journal is perfect for beginners curious about the Law of Attraction and for long-time journal-lovers on the search for something different.

Divided into four main sections—success, health, relationships, and inner wisdom—this journal will teach you about the 24 Diamond Energy Practices and how you can use them to transform every aspect of your life. Each chapter comes with a range of thought-provoking journal questions, engaging practical tasks, and Feng Shui tips.

So, whether you want to attract a new career or bring back that spark of passion to your relationship, this carefully curated journal will teach you how to use Diamond Energy in order to manifest the life of your dreams, one page at a time!

ACKNOWLEDGMENTS

Firstly, I would like to thank Jean, my husband, and my children Anthony, Ace, and Enya. They have walked alongside me on this journey and have supported me in manifesting my vision to enlighten more than 500 million people. I would also like to thank all my students from the last 30 years from all over the world. By sharing this wisdom with their own families and those around them, they are playing an important part in enlightening the world, too.

I would like to thank Hay House for their unwavering support, guidance, and belief in me throughout this exciting new chapter in my life. I would like to thank Cassandra Cooper, my business partner and producer on the *Feng Shui Your Life* TV series, for her tremendous hard work and for helping bring my vision to life.

I would like to thank Vishen Lakhiani and the Mindvalley community, Pablo Farias and the YouUnity community, and Pete Bissonnette and all the Learning Strategies students. I would also like to thank Rhonda Byrne, the producer and author of *The Secret*, for giving me the chance to share my teachings with the world.

Finally, I would like to thank my Diamond Team for being there to support me every step of the way.

About the Author

Marie Diamond is a world-renowned Master Teacher of Feng Shui and the Law of Attraction, and the star of the major network TV series *Feng Shui Your Life*. She also featured in the global movie phenomenon *The Secret*.

Marie has taught more than one million students over the last 30 years and has spoken in more than 30 different countries. She is a personal, business, and spiritual mentor and consultant to celebrities in the film and music industry and top entrepreneurs worldwide. For her humanitarian work, she is a knighted Dame.

@mariediamondofficial

www.mariediamond.com

We hope you enjoyed this Hay House book. If you'd like to receive our online catalog featuring additional information on Hay House books and products, or if you'd like to find out more about the Hay Foundation, please contact:

Hay House, Inc., P.O. Box 5100, Carlsbad, CA 92018-5100
(760) 431-7695 or (800) 654-5126
(760) 431-6948 (fax) or (800) 650-5115 (fax)
www.hayhouse.com® • www.hayfoundation.org

———

Published in Australia by: Hay House Australia Pty. Ltd.,
18/36 Ralph St., Alexandria NSW 2015
Phone: 612-9669-4299 • *Fax:* 612-9669-4144
www.hayhouse.com.au

Published in the United Kingdom by: Hay House UK, Ltd.,
The Sixth Floor, Watson House, 54 Baker Street, London W1U 7BU
Phone: +44 (0)20 3927 7290 • *Fax:* +44 (0)20 3927 7291
www.hayhouse.co.uk

Published in India by: Hay House Publishers India,
Muskaan Complex, Plot No. 3, B-2, Vasant Kunj, New Delhi 110 070
Phone: 91-11-4176-1620 • *Fax:* 91-11-4176-1630
www.hayhouse.co.in

———

CONNECT WITH

HAY HOUSE

ONLINE

🌐 hayhouse.co.uk   **f** @hayhouse

📷 @hayhouseuk   🐦 @hayhouseuk

▶ @hayhouseuk   ♪ @hayhouseuk

Find out all about our latest books & card decks • Be the first to know about exclusive discounts • Interact with our authors in live broadcasts • Celebrate the cycle of the seasons with us • Watch free videos from your favourite authors • Connect with like-minded souls

'*The gateways to wisdom and knowledge are always open.*'

Louise Hay